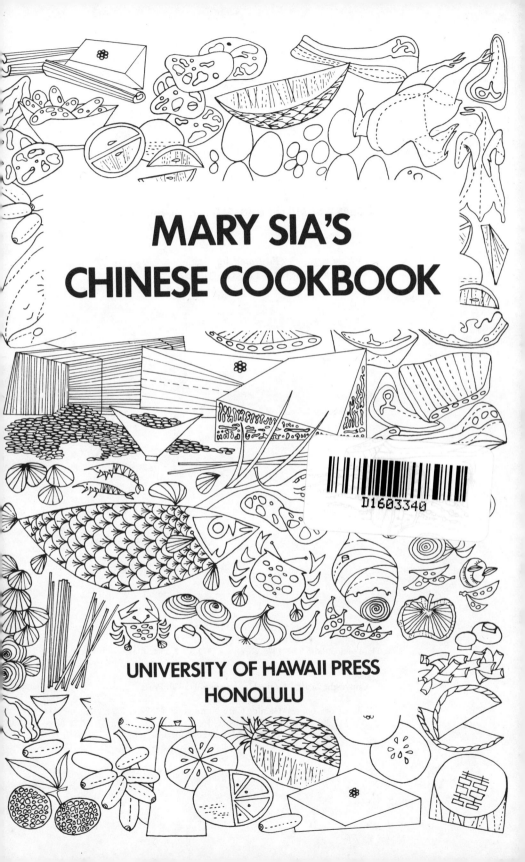

MARY SIA'S
CHINESE COOKBOOK

UNIVERSITY OF HAWAII PRESS
HONOLULU

Background Material by
ROBERT S. MILNE and ALDYTH V. MORRIS

Illustrated by
CLEMENTE LAGUNDIMAO

First edition 1956
Second edition 1957, 1959, 1961
Third edition 1964, 1967, 1972; paperback 1975, 1977, 1980, 1984

食譜

謝李靈生著

記念
我甚愛的母親：
李江氏醫學博士

To my beloved mother
DR. TAI HEONG KONG LI

FOREWORD

引
言

I have always held with Bernard Shaw that "there is no love sincerer than the love of food," only I would make it "*exotic* food." Given this basic philosophy of life, it was inevitable that I would some day find myself enrolled in Mrs. Sia's famous Chinese cooking class. The date was 1951, spring, and I was the sole male in a class of twenty-four! My embarrassment was not lessened when my classmates, assuming a total ignorance of cooking fundamentals on my part, would not even let me break my own eggs and open my own cans! Eventually, they accepted me as an equal, and I must say that we had a jolly time learning to make some of the more mouth-watering dishes of both north and south China. At lunchtime, our cooking chores done, we would sit down to enjoy the fruit of our handiwork—Lucullan feasts featuring simple dishes like Fried Rice, Egg Fu Yung, and Pineapple Spareribs with Sweet-Sour Sauce, and slightly more complicated dishes like Walnut Chicken, Eight Precious Pudding, and that extra delicious Peking dish, *Chiao Tzu* (meat dumplings). Never have I eaten better! But Mrs. Sia taught us a good deal more than how to prepare selected, tasty, authentic dishes. She imparted to us something of the "philosophy" of Chinese cooking—what different foods symbolize, for example. It was an enchanting experience—so much so that I repeated the course in 1952, again the only male in a class of two dozen!

Some time afterward, I had this inspiration. Not everybody has the leisure of a university professor, but there must be many who would like to do the next best thing to sitting at Mrs. Sia's feet, namely, to read a book by her on the Chinese way of cooking. I made this suggestion to the University of Hawaii Press, and herewith is the result.

Dr. Johnson felt that "women cannot make a good book of cookery." To see how far off base the good Doctor was, you must read Mrs. Sia's book, with its choice, classroom-tested recipes and her knowledge of the lore and charm of one of the great schools of world cookery.

And now, men and women, to *wock* and chopsticks!

ARTHUR J. MARDER

Honolulu, Hawaii

PREFACE

序   Good food is the essence of good living. The Chinese, ever seeking good living, insist on the pleasing of the palate. Being Chinese, I have sought the ultimate in cooking in the Chinese way. Enthusiast that I am, I have spent a lifetime in opening new culinary worlds to thousands of people, both in the East and in the West.

My mother, Dr. T. H. Kong Li, was a medical doctor with a zest for living. Her love of life attracted guests from every part of the world and her warm hospitality included the finest Chinese food. In this atmosphere, my interest in the art of Chinese cooking naturally took root and flourished.

After earning a degree in home economics from the University of Hawaii, I pursued graduate studies in the same field at Cornell University. Marriage to a research physician, whose work carried him to Peking, China, in 1924, meant that I found myself in the heart of China's cultural center, where there was also an abundance of restaurants serving the specialties of the many sections of China. Here, indeed, was the ideal laboratory in which to taste traditional Chinese dishes and test them in the light of western home economics. Here, I conducted my first Chinese cooking classes, which developed into the Restaurant Study Group of the Peiping International Women's Club.

I was soon deluged with requests for a Chinese cookbook in English. The Chinese, like many Europeans, rarely bother to measure out ingredients and condiments in terms of cups and tablespoons; it is always "a pinch of this" or "a dash of that." I found that behind the art of Chinese cooking is its science. This provided the necessary inspiration for my book *Chinese Chopsticks,* published in 1935. It sold out rapidly, and a second edition appeared in 1938.

I returned to Hawaii shortly thereafter, and resumed my instruction in Chinese cooking by starting a new series of classes at the Honolulu YWCA. There I derived great satisfaction from transmitting to thousands of women—and men, too—the background for practicing the delicate art of palate-pleasing in the Chinese way. Continuous requests for a cookbook have resulted in the present work.

Of the many who have helped in the preparation of this book, I want especially to thank my sister Li Ling Ai, my daughter-in-law Katherine Li Sia, William S. Ellis, Jr., who designed it, and my good friends Professor Arthur Marder and editors Aldyth Morris and Robert Milne.

Mary Li Sia

Honolulu, Hawaii

CONTENTS

INTRODUCTION

概
論

Eating, gambling, and theatre-going have been called the three national vices of China. Also it has been said that the Chinese may not be serious about their religion or their learning, but they are certainly serious about their cooking. While both statements may be exaggerations, still it is true that China is a land of epicures. Biographies of great men include descriptions of their eating habits, and novels dwell on the pleasures of the table. It is said that Confucius, for whom "rice never could be white enough," left his wife because she was not a good cook. Obviously, in China the joys of eating are openly acknowledged and cooking has become an art.

Many factors have combined to cause the Chinese to develop their own particular cooking techniques. One of these is the ever-present scarcity of fuel. An American missionary is credited with saying that in China a straw will not tell you which way the wind blows—before the wind has had a chance to blow, someone will have picked up the straw and carried it home for fuel. After a windstorm it is common to see people in the streets gathering the broken twigs and branches to be used as fuel. There is even a kind of burglar who goes about with a knife on a long pole lopping off branches of trees to be sold as firewood. In the fall, before the frost has withered the grass, families turn to and strip the hillsides, bringing home the precious bundles of grass to be dried and used for fuel.

This need to conserve fuel has influenced the kind of crops

raised for food, the methods of preparing and cooking them, and even the shape and thickness of pots and pans. It explains, in part at least, why rice is the staple starch in most of China—it takes less fuel to steam a pot of rice than it does to bake a loaf of bread. It also explains why there are few roasted or baked dishes and why so much time is spent in preparing food.

This shortage of fuel has also tended to make China the home of caterers and delicatessens. Some of the poorer families prepare only a few items at home—rice, a vegetable or two, and tea. They buy the rest from peddlers who cry their wares from door to door, or at shops where quantity production makes it possible to sell for less than the cost of home cooking. Even water heated to temperatures varying from tepid to boiling may be bought from shops or peddlers.

Another factor which has influenced the cooking and eating habits of China is the frequent threat of famine. Poverty and food shortages have driven people to experiment with everything edible, with the result that the Chinese diet includes items which the Westerner has considered inedible, as well as many he had never thought of using as food. Chrysanthemum petals and dried golden lily buds, for instance, are among the ingredients called for in the recipes which follow.

Poverty and shortage have also taught the Chinese to avoid waste. Bones are simmered to make stock. The liquor from canned vegetables, the water in which vegetables have been par-boiled, and the second water in which dried ingredients have been soaked are used as substitutes in recipes calling for plain water. Even the water in which meat dumplings have been cooked is seasoned and served as broth.

The Chinese cook is an artist who strives to heighten the color, retain the original texture, enhance the natural flavor, mask undesirable qualities, and achieve a pleasant uniformity in the size and shape of the ingredients which go into a particular dish. He calculates time to the second, and will prepare and cook ingredients separately rather than destroy the color or crispness of vegetables or toughen the meat by overcooking.

Color and texture are preserved by cooking only what is fresh and tender and by serving it immediately. Knowing the symbolic meaning of colors, a Chinese cook will tramp blocks to find a bright red pepper so that the joy color may be introduced into his recipe. A Chinese hostess will create a dish which harmonizes with her china or her gown, but it must also taste delicious and be suitable to the occasion.

Natural flavors may be enhanced by combining foods which complement each other or by the judicious use of sauces, spices, and other flavoring agents. Some comparatively tasteless foods are highly nutritious and combine well with others. *Taofu,* for instance, combined with meat dishes adds bulk and nourishment and at the same time absorbs the flavor of the meat.

The different ingredients of a dish are usually of uniform size and shape and cut small enough to be eaten in one bite. If a recipe calls for peas or corn the other ingredients are usually cubed. If bean sprouts are an important item the others are shredded. This explains why chopsticks and a porcelain spoon are usually the only service needed at a Chinese table.

THE CHINESE FEAST

中
國
盛
饌

The feast is the principal social function in China. It combines the best features of the Western cocktail party and banquet without the unpleasant features of either. Instead of standing around, drink in hand, until they are intoxicated, the guests at a Chinese feast are seated at round tables shortly after they arrive. The purpose of the feast is to enjoy each other's company, and, since the tables are round, anyone can talk to anyone else and usually does. The guests drink wine from tiny cups and eat bites of food at the same time, and good fellowship is achieved without intoxication.

As soon as the happy mood is set people move from one seat to another, with all the freedom of a cocktail party. Literary games, wine games, and personal interchange keep the party on a lively plane. The gaiety may be sustained for hours – in sharp contrast to the atmosphere surrounding a Western banquet where the guests, gorged with food and drink, sit hours in discomfort and boredom listening to long speeches.

At a dinner party in a home, wine is warmed as soon as the guests arrive. The Chinese say, "No wine, no conversation; no conversation, no company." Most Chinese love company, therefore they love wine. It is always served in pots of shining brass, floral porcelain, or pewter.

As the guests enter the dining room, the host announces the name of the guest of honor, fills his cup with wine, indicates his seat, then does the same for all the other guests. The guest of honor returns the compliment by filling his host's cup. When all the guests are seated, the host sits down. He raises his cup and says, *"Ch'ing"* ("Please"). The guests raise their cups and say, *"Hsieh, hsieh"* ("Many thanks for your hospitality"), then everyone drinks.

Many an American housewife who frets while her guests continue drinking as the dinner gets cold would enjoy the Chinese system of cutting off the "cocktail hour." When the host feels there has been enough drinking for the time being, he simply picks up a pair of chopsticks and says, *"Ch'ing,"* then the guest of honor starts eating as a signal for all to begin. Often during the course of the meal the host will say *"Kan pei!"* ("Empty cup!"), and everyone empties his cup. Wine is usually served whenever a new dish is placed on the table. By alternately serving food and wine, the host keeps his guests happy, yet prevents intoxication.

Even though a guest might not desire wine, he usually sips a bit of it. In Peiping, a teetotaler who refuses to touch wine is called *mien pi,* which means "facing the wall."

On a special occasion, such as a wedding banquet, where the guests are seated at several tables, the host visits each table with a cup of wine in his hand and drinks with the guests. The first main dish at each table is served in the presence of the host. This is called "presenting." Guests thank the host and drink with him immediately after the "presentation," then they start eating while the host goes to the next table.

No wine is served after the last course of the meal. A servant passes hot towels, moist and scented, on a tray. These take the place of the Western finger bowl and napkin, and are also refreshing when applied to the face. When a guest has finished with his towel, it is proper procedure for him to *throw* it to the servant. The towels signal the end of the evening.

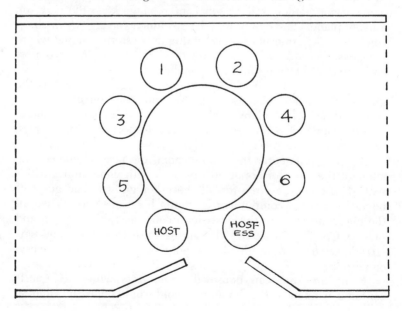

The table setting for a Chinese meal, formal or informal, is simple, consisting of a pair of chopsticks, a porcelain spoon, a bowl for soup or rice, a medium-sized plate, a saucer, and a tiny cup for tea.

The host and hostess sit together in the least desirable seats — with their backs to the door. The guests of honor are seated directly opposite them, facing the door. The others are seated according to rank, the most important on either side of the guests of honor, the least important next to the host and hostess.

Both tea and wine are important in the social and ceremonial life of China.

TEA AS A BEVERAGE

茶爲飲料之一

Tea is the national beverage of China and is taken by all kinds of people in all kinds of ways. The laborer gulps strong, hot tea in big pots to restore his strength. The connoisseur spends infinite care, preparing tea with meticulous exactitude amid carefully chosen surroundings so the taste will be exactly right and the atmosphere will be most conducive to its enjoyment. He sips his tea slowly, to savor the delicate taste and aroma. He can tell from a sip how much the tea cost, how it was cured, and how much time elapsed after the water stopped boiling and before it was poured over the leaves. Between the laborer and the connoisseur are all the other people of China, to whom tea brings simple refreshment and an opportunity for pleasant relaxation and conversation.

The legends concerning the origin of tea are many. One says that Bodhidharma, a Buddhist saint, went from India to China about A.D. 519, with the intention of mortifying his flesh, living an exemplary life, and teaching the Chinese about Buddha. He lived on wild herbs and denied himself any rest. One night, wearied beyond control, he fell asleep. On waking, he was ashamed of having broken his vow. To do penance, he cut off his eyelids and threw them on the ground. The next day each eyelid had become a bush, the first tea plants on earth. Bodhidharma, upon eating the leaves, found that his heart was filled with joy and that his soul gained new strength and energy to continue his contemplation.

Another legend says that an early emperor, in order to prevent disease caused by impure water, decreed that his troops drink only boiled water. The soldiers discovered that tea leaves made the hot water palatable. Thus commenced the use of tea. This is perhaps close to the truth, although it probably happened in India. Tea was actually introduced into China from India about the time of Bodhidharma, in the sixth century, and within two hundred years it had become a universal beverage.

Tea grows on ground that won't support any edible crop, a fact which undoubtedly contributed to its spread in land-hungry China. It is planted in otherwise useless areas around houses, on hillsides above the rice paddies, and high in the mountains. The quality of tea is improved by the clouds, snow, and misty atmosphere of high altitudes.

The farmer plants tea seeds in September and waits three years for his first harvest. In a wild state, tea becomes a tree, but like olive trees in Mediterranean countries, it is kept trimmed to a height of five feet or less, in order to make picking easy and to concentrate the energy of the plant in production rather than in height.

The tea leaves are picked in April, May, and August. The tree produces small crops until it is six years old, a full crop by the tenth year, and good leaves for another ten years. The April picking, when the leaves are covered with down, gives the best crop, and is called pekoe tea. The picking has to be completed within three to five days to prevent the leaves from becoming tough. The higher the leaves are on the bush, the better their quality.

The difference between green teas and black teas (called red teas in China) is that in black teas the chlorophyll is chemically altered by fermentation before drying, while green teas are dried in the sun or in drying rooms where they may also be steamed. Processes vary considerably.

The tea leaves have to be curled, to help release the juices. This is done by coolies crushing the leaves in tubs with their feet, or by hand, or in crimping machines.

After sorting and blending, the leaves are packed in chests lined with lead or pewter foil. Some teas, particularly the heavy and medicinal ones, are sold in bricks, made by pulverizing the leaves, steaming the "tea dust," and compressing it into hard cakes. There is no clear distinction between food and medicine, and the different teas can be classified as simple refreshment, as tonics, or as medicines, according to strength and composition.

Many Chinese teas have dried flowers or leaves packed with them, to impart flavor, fragrance, and the idyllic thought that one is sipping nectar. Those used include chrysanthemums, roses, orange blossoms, jasmine, camellias, and various buds and aromatic leaves.

Certain teas are considered "warming," and others "cooling," even though both are served piping hot. During China's hot summers, mountain green teas and such flower teas as yellow chrysanthemum are used, while in winter the heavier black teas are preferred. There is a tea for every mood and every kind of guest or friend. Flower tea enhances the pleasure of reading poetry, herb tea improves the health, and a light, clear tea soothes the mind and body.

When tea became the national drink for Great Britain and many of her colonies, it brought great wealth to the tea exporters of Foochow. In 1814, China was exporting about ten million dollars' worth of tea each year, but in 1850 the trade was only half that, and by 1930 it was down to almost nothing. The teas of India had become more popular outside of China.

Indian tea is stronger and more astringent than Chinese tea, and this seems to be preferred in the West. Occidentals allow a spoonful of tea leaves for each cup. This makes the strong stimulant desired in the West, but to the Chinese it seems bitter and unpleasant. Naturally, it requires sugar with milk or lemon to make it palatable.

The Chinese use only one teaspoonful of tea leaves to six cups of boiling water. This produces a lightly refreshing pale golden drink with a delicate flavor, and the addition of milk, sugar, or lemon is considered a barbarous pollution. Except for the occasional use of flowers, the Chinese almost never add any flavoring to a cup of tea. Chinese connoisseurs of tea are meticulous, perhaps even more so than connoisseurs of wine in Europe. They insist, for instance, that tea must never be brewed in the kitchen, where it might take on odors to spoil its fragrance, or become contaminated with oil or other foods. Their tea cups and other paraphernalia must be washed apart from other dishes, and must never be wiped with a cloth. They demand absolute adherence to form, including the requirement that the water be heated to a precise point of turbulence known as the "third boil," that there be no more than three or four guests, that the pot be the right size for the number of people present, that it be scalded properly before using, and so forth. They vie with each other in attempts to produce the most esthetic cup of tea. One says the best tea is made from mountain spring water, another requires water collected from lotus leaves on a pond, a third claims that snow must be melted for the perfect water, and there are those who insist that only from collected dew can perfect tea be brewed.

A guest is always offered tea upon arrival, no matter what the time of day or night. Afternoon callers are usually served almond or rice cakes, preserved ginger, or shrimp chips with their tea. Even restaurants serve tea as soon as the guest sits down. There is a standard charge for this.

There is a story that a host who had invited a visitor to have tea was dismayed when the water was boiling but the servant sent to borrow tea leaves had not returned. The host's wife suggested that since the water was hot and there was no tea, he offer his guest a bath instead of a cup of tea.

Tea is kept hot all day in offices and homes, typically in a large porcelain pot kept warm in a basket whose thick inner padding is made to fit the pot. This is of course "ordinary" tea When tea is to be prepared for special guests, the water is carefully selected and kept in the right kind of pot, one or more special stoves are employed, special servants may be detailed to make tea, the best chinaware is used, and the tea is brewed in the cup.

The formal tea service requires that each person have a saucer, cup, and lid. The tea leaves are placed in the bottom of the cup, the boiling water is poured in, and the lid put on to keep the tea warm and to cover the leaves. The lid floats just below the surface and is left in the cup while the tea is drunk, thus keeping the leaves out of the mouth. The first cup is considered a bit immature, the second cup is best, and the third cup from the same leaves is also good.

Tea is ceremonially served on many occasions in Chinese life. One of these is at marriage. Before leaving her parents' home, the bride personally pours and serves tea in cups of red (for joy) to all her relatives, her husband's relatives, and the other guests, in the strict order of their importance at the ceremony. After her brother, her maid, and the matchmaker escort her in a red sedan chair to the groom's house, she is served tea containing dates, peanuts, dragon nuts, and lotus seeds. The names of these ingredients have the same sound as the phrase, "Early-born precious son." Also, at Chinese New Year, guests are offered tea containing sweet preserved fruits such as melon, lotus seed, lotus root, and dates, to symbolize the wish that the year will be filled with sweetness.

Besides being used as a beverage any time during the day, at home, at work, and even in the midst of theater performances, tea is always served before and after meals. The southern Chinese may drink tea throughout the meal, but in north China the only part of the meal accompanied by tea is dessert. Two of the special teas often served with dessert are Tit-koon-yum and Tit-lo-hon.

These leaves are grown on mountain cliffs by monks, who train monkeys to scale the cliffs and fill their baskets with leaves. These teas are always served in individual four-inch-high teapots and drunk from very small teacups. In preparing the tea, each pot, filled to the brim with tea leaves, is placed in a bowl. Boiling water is poured into the bowl to warm the pot and the leaves. After a few minutes, boiling water is poured into the teapot and the tea is allowed to steep. The first pot is always bitter, but is drunk to show that one can endure the bitterness of life. The fourth pot, using the same leaves, is the best. At this point, the tea is sipped very slowly, so that it leaves a delicate flavor in the mouth. Another tea picked by monkeys is the green Cloud Mist tea, which grows on the mountain tops of Kiangsi.

China has more kinds of tea than Europe has wines, and every subtle difference is a new delight to be savored to the fullest. This idealization of tea is certainly more practical than that of wine, since intemperate use of tea can only make the drinker tired of it (although certain extremists have gone bankrupt through drinking highly exotic and expensive teas), while intemperate use of wine and liquors has far more disagreeable results.

Just as the coffeehouses of eighteenth-century England, France, and America were centers for gossip, gambling, political intrigue, and the discussion of art and literature, so the teahouses of China have been places where all sorts of people drop in for a snack and some lively conversation or the leisurely transaction of business.

There are teahouses for all the different classes. Those for rickshawmen and laborers are furnished with rough benches and tables. Tea is sold in thick cups or bowls, and peanuts and melon seeds are also for sale. In many a lower-class teashop there is a platform for a professional storyteller. He sits for several hours, telling a serialized story, and every ten or fifteen minutes stops until a collection of money has made it worth while to continue.

The most luxurious teashops are set in cool places of natural beauty or historic interest. In Peiping there are many scattered along the lakes and in the parks. One of the best is on the marble boat at the Summer Palace. This boat is sometimes called "China's navy," since the Empress built it with money allocated for the establishment of a navy. These elegant teashops serve light lunches and fancy cakes, dumplings, and sweetmeats. Their patrons while away whole summer afternoons or evenings in conversation over their tea.

There are hundreds of well-known varieties of tea. Most of them come from the same kind of bush, the difference in taste being due to the location in which the bush grows, the time of year at which the leaves are picked, the position of the leaves on the bush, the way they are prepared before packing, and the way the infusion is made.

Dragon Well tea is a slightly bitter blend of green teas from the West Lake in Hangchow, in the province of Chekiang which also produces the black Woo Loong (Five Dragon) tea. Iron Goddess of Mercy tea comes from Fukien, is quite thick, and is served in very small cups. Black Dragon is a black tea from Kwangtung. Mulberry is a green tea made with young mulberry leaves. Powchow, a green tea from north China, has the smell of new-mown hay. Su-tang is a black tea with a smoky flavor, grown in Fukien.

Dragon's Whiskers tea is a lightly colored and delicately flavored green tea, the only variety of tea sold in small packages in China. Lo-cha is an Oolong tea from Formosa. It is semi-fermented, producing a mild amber brew. Some of the green teas from Kwangtung are Water Nymph, Eyebrows of Longevity, and Silver Needles. The black Clear Distance tea is also from Kwangtung. Lychee is a green tea very popular with Cantonese. Like other fruit teas, it is served in summer. Black Wu-I tea from Yunnan is very bitter and is used as a medicine for colds. There are countless other varieties.

Americans in China generally prefer the scented flower teas, but each type has its adherents. Trying them and learning the good points of each can lead to a series of happy minor adventures of the kind frequently indulged in by the Chinese. When the occidental has discovered the pleasure to be found in this kind of experience he has come a long way towards understanding the Chinese enjoyment of life.

To make tea, first rinse the pot with rapidly boiling water, then drop in the leaves. (One teaspoon of leaves to six cups of water will make an infusion delicately flavored and without bitterness.) Pour water which has been brought to a boil and has reached its maximum agitation over the leaves and let steep. The time required for steeping varies according to the type of tea, the amount of leaves in relation to the amount of water, individual taste, but the average length of time is three minutes.

It is good manners in China to show appreciation by making plenty of noise while sipping tea—a custom which sometimes startles Westerners.

WINE AS A BEVERAGE

酒爲飲料之一

Wine originated, according to an old tale, when a chef of the imperial palace put some rice to soak in an earthen crock and completely forgot about it. Several days later he discovered the crock and tried the rice to see if it had spoiled. The rice was delicious, and the liquid was even better. He drank some more and soon broke into joyous song.

The news of this remarkable discovery was reported to the emperor, who tried a large sample himself. He, too, was delighted and stimulated. He ordered a large supply of the liquid prepared, and issued invitations to a very special feast. It was a great success, and the emperor discovered that after a few drinks, stubborn opponents became quite amenable to his point of view.

However, the next morning when the emperor held audience — it was customary to start the transaction of state business before daybreak — he found himself alone, for the wine had put his officials in a condition beyond caring about business. The emperor meditated, then promulgated rules for drinking: (1) Wine must be served in very small cups, not soup bowls. (2) No one should drink on an empty stomach and food must be taken with the wine. (3) Drinkers must engage in a mild form of physical exercise and must also keep their minds busy, which probably explains the popularity of such games as "guessing fingers."

"Guessing fingers" is an energetic and noisy game in which two players simultaneously fling out their right fists, pointing a number of fingers, while at the same time each one shouts out his guess as to what the total number of fingers will be. It must be done in rhythm, so it sounds like a song or football cheer. The guessing continues until one player guesses the correct number of fingers extended. The loser, as a forfeit, must take a drink of wine, then the game goes on. As more wine is consumed, the players shout their numbers more and more loudly. The game may go on for hours. The object is to remain sober and to force one's opponent to lose his wits. The one who gets drunk loses face, while the winner is called a *hai liang*, a person with the capacity of the sea.

A large capacity for alcohol has been a traditional source of pride among Chinese poets and writers for many centuries. Over a thousand years ago, Huang-fu Sung wrote, "The man of refinement should strive to increase the number of rounds he can stand and so add to the number of his conquests and increase his prestige."

Wang Chi could hold so much that he is still known as "the

Five-Bottle Scholar." Liu Ling, president of "The Seven Sages of the Bamboo Grove" in A.D. 300, was always followed by two servants, one carrying a bottle of wine and the other bearing a shovel with which to bury Liu Ling where he fell if he should die of drink.

The great poet Li Po, who ends one of his poems, "The rapture of drinking, and wine's dizzy joy, No man who is sober deserves," was banished by his emperor for continual drunkenness. He died of drink and drowning, having fallen out of a boat while trying to embrace the moon's reflection in a lotus pool. T'ao Ch'ien (A.D. 365–429), recognized as China's greatest poet in the five-word meter, used wine to soothe his mind and free his emotions so he could write.

Literary drinkers were called "Drunken Dragons," and because of the general reverence for poetry and writing they were permitted debauchery which would not be tolerated among other people.

In the thirteenth century, Chu Hsi wrote several volumes of instructions for the young, called *Siao Hio*. Taking his precepts straight from the *Analects*, he says that a limit cannot be set beforehand to the amount of wine one should drink, because wine brings harmony and peace among men; but one must not drink enough to cause drunkenness and trouble. Confucius himself, however, admitted with irony and regret that he was occasionally "overcome by wine."

The Imperial Cookery Book of the Mongol Dynasty gives fifteen rules for drinking, which include some sensible advice as well as some superstition. Rule thirteen is, "When drunk, don't get so excited that you scare your soul out of your body for good."

Despite the "Drunken Dragons" and the many poems and essays about drinking, however, the Chinese in general are a most temperate race. They use wine to increase good fellowship — but they almost always have enough food and light exercise with the wine to prevent real drunkenness. The scholars and poets sing the praises of wine, but this is more a literary convention than an accurate report of their actions. As Lin Yutang says, many writers have "the sentiment for wine" without having a real desire or capacity for it.

"Wine doesn't intoxicate men. Men intoxicate themselves." This is but one of many similar proverbs showing the care with which the Chinese control their drinking. Another says, "At the first glass, the man drinks the wine; at the second glass the wine drinks the wine; at the third glass the wine drinks the man."

A pleasant old family custom in Peking was to take wine and cups and walk out to temples and scenic places in the countryside on holidays in warm weather. Sometimes the person pouring the wine would float half-filled cups down a meandering stream to the others, making a game of it and increasing their anticipation. In the courts of certain temples and homes are intricate artificial watercourses in the outline of beasts and birds, especially constructed to make the journey of a wine cup tortuous and tantalizing.

Marco Polo reported six hundred years ago, "The greater part of the inhabitants of the province of Cathay drink a sort of wine made from rice mixed with a variety of spices and drugs. This beverage, or wine as it may be termed, is so good and well flavored that they do not wish for better. It is clear, bright and pleasant to the taste, and being very hot, has the quality of inebriating sooner than any other."

There are two main kinds of wine in China, yellow and white. The *vin ordinaire* throughout most of the country is *shaohsing*, a yellow rice wine like sherry which is made in Shaohsingfu, Chekiang province, and in many other places. It is used for cooking as well as for drinking, and serves for both ceremonial and special occasions. It is usually heated before serving. In restaurants, *shaohsing* is usually warmed in a double boiler, then served in wine pots; but at home it comes before the guests in a small wine pot immersed in a shell of wood filled with hot water. In and around the city of Shaohsing, it is the custom when a daughter is born to make a jar of wine and bury it so that when she marries, her dowry will include some valuable and well-aged wine.

Shantung is a yellow wine made in Peking. Five Companies wine, also yellow, is from Canton. It is very strong, flavored with spices, and is thought to aid the circulation of the blood. Five Companies is sometimes used in cooking steamed chicken and pork, but *shaohsing* is preferred because it is not as strong.

The chief white wine is *kaoliang*, made from the purple-topped grain of that name in the north of China. This is comparable to vodka in strength and flavor, and is the beverage most frequently used on those occasions when *shaohsing* is not considered strong enough. Other white wines are "tiger tendon and quince wine," a strong drink served to elderly people with the hope of relieving rheumatism; rose petal wine, which is high in alcoholic content, is flavored with rose petals and is as fragrant as a bouquet; and two mild white wines: pear wine and orange wine.

Solitary drinking is frowned upon in China, just as it is in the West. It does occur, of course, but this is considered a perversion of the true function of wine, which is to stimulate social intercourse. The Chinese version of Alcoholics Anonymous is the *Li Men* (Door of Reason Society). There are chapters in most large cities. The problem is attacked with lectures, with prostration and prayers to Buddha and Kwan Yin, and the use of a black pasty mixture which is supposed to kill the desire for alcohol.

Wine is often used to honor the dead. In the *san ch'i* (three times seven) ceremony, held three weeks after the day death occurred, the best wine available is presented along with the deceased's favorite foods. These are spread out early in the morning on a square table placed on the bed of the deceased. His spirit supposedly comes to enjoy the food and drink in a reunion with his family. There are also many ceremonies during the year when bowls of food and cups of wine are placed on the graves of the dead, especially one's ancestors.

Toward the end of the chamber ceremony in a Chinese wedding, two small cups, tied together at the handles with red cord, are presented to the bride and groom. The go-between (who has arranged the marriage bargain) pours wine into the two cups from two pots which are similarly tied together. The bride and groom sip a bit of this wine, then the go-between pours some wine from the groom's cup into the bride's, and some from hers into his. They exchange cups and drink some of the mingled wine, symbolizing the intermingling of their own bodies and spirits.

COOKING METHODS

烹
飪
術

The distinctiveness of Chinese cooking derives from both the methods and materials used, and no Chinese cookbook would be complete without a brief description of both.

PREPARATION

As a rule, a maximum amount of time is spent in preparation and, since fuel is scarce, a minimum in cooking. Ingredients are sliced, diced, minced, marinated, and even cooked, separately, then combined quickly into a delectable dish. Some of the terms used to describe the preparation of the ingredients are defined below.

Chop. To cut into small pieces without regard to shape, usually done with two cleavers, one in each hand.

Cube. To cut into ½-inch cubes.

Crush. To reduce to fine particles by pounding or by the use of pressure. Garlic or ginger may be crushed with the broad side of a cleaver.

Dice. To cut into ¼-inch cubes.

Marinate. To soak food in a sauce to improve its flavor. The sauce in which food has been soaked is called the *marinade.*

Mince. To chop very fine.

Shred. To cut into very thin strips. To shred meat, cut in long pieces about 1 inch wide and ½ inch thick. Slice diagonally, then cut slices into thin strips.

Slice. To cut into thin, flat pieces, usually across the grain. There are two ways of slicing—straight and diagonal. For purposes of slicing and parboiling (see page 17), vegetables may be divided into groups:

(1) Hard vegetables: broccoli, cauliflower, carrots, string beans.

(2) Semi-hard vegetables: bamboo shoots, bitter melon, celery cabbage, Chinese peas, lotus root, mustard cabbage, peas, turnips.

(3) Soft vegetables: bean sprouts, bell peppers, celery, head cabbage, cucumbers, eggplant, lettuce, mushrooms, okra, green onions, round onions, parsley, radishes, spinach, tomatoes, water chestnuts, water cress.

The harder vegetables and the coarse-grained meats are usually sliced diagonally, exposing a larger surface for the action of heat and for the absorption of flavors. Softer vegetables are

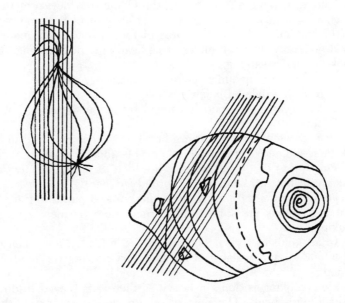

usually sliced straight across. Fragile vegetables, such as green onions, parsley, spinach, and water cress may be cut to the desired lengths with kitchen scissors.

Following are a few tips on slicing:

Cut peeled carrots and turnips into 2-inch lengths, then slice diagonally.

Cut the top and bottom off a round onion, then cut it in two lengthwise. Remove skins. Place onion halves flat side down and slice crosswise.

Broccoli stems should be peeled, then sliced diagonally. If stems are very large they should be cut in two lengthwise before slicing.

Cut head cabbage into quarters, then slice quarters crosswise.

Peel water chestnuts and slice crosswise.

Peel lotus root and cut crosswise into slices of the desired thickness.

Cut peeled Chinese yam lengthwise into thick pieces. Slice each piece diagonally.

Cut bamboo shoots lengthwise into pieces ½ inch thick. Slice diagonally.

COOKING

As mentioned earlier, the ever-present scarcity of fuel and the threat of famine have taught the Chinese to devise methods of cooking which require the smallest amount of fuel and result in the minimum shrinkage or loss of food values. The methods most generally used fall under three headings: fast cooking, slow cooking, and steaming.

Fast cooking includes boiling, simmering, and the various ways of frying defined below:

Deep frying. The food is cooked by immersing it in hot oil until done.

Fricasseeing. Ingredients are first browned or pan fried in hot oil, then simmered in a small amount of sauce or stock.

Pan frying or *quick frying.* The food is fried lightly and quickly in hot fat, while being turned frequently.

Sautéing or *stir frying* is much the same as pan frying except that ingredients are stirred and turned more frequently during cooking.

In all kinds of frying the pan is usually heated first, then the oil is added, and when it is hot and easy-flowing the foods are added.

Slow cooking is done in heavy earthen pots placed in direct contact with heat. The pots warm up slowly but retain their heat a long time, so there is no waste of fuel. This is a favorite method of cooking rice.

Steaming consists of exposing the food either directly or indirectly to the action of steam. Americans usually employ the indirect or dry-steam method of cooking over boiling water, as in a double boiler. The Chinese usually follow the direct or wet-steam method, and have devised two kinds of steamers (see Cooking Utensils, page 22–23). Rice, dumplings, buns, hash, and many other dishes are steam cooked.

Vegetables are frequently parboiled before being further cooked in combination with other ingredients. The water should be boiling and should be kept boiling for the length of time indicated. Unless instructions are given to the contrary, hard vegetables should be parboiled 1½ minutes and semi-hard ½ minute. Soft vegetables, such as bean sprouts, should be dropped into the boiling water and removed almost at once. (See page 15 for list of hard, semi-hard, and soft vegetables.)

MATERIALS

烹
飪
器
具

The threat of food shortage has compelled the Chinese to find ways of preserving every morsel of food not consumed in its fresh state. Hence the wide variety of candied, dried, salted, and pickled foods called for in Chinese recipes.

Many people, tasting Chinese food for the first time, will ask wistfully, "What gives it that mysterious flavor?" or "What is that crisp crunchy vegetable?" When such flavoring agents as fish extract or pressed bean curd fermented in wine are mentioned, or such vegetables as bamboo shoots and water chestnuts, or such dried ingredients as fungi or golden lily buds, many refuse to believe that they can either obtain the materials or learn the technique of Chinese cooking.

Yet, with a little persistence and ingenuity almost anyone can prepare authentic Chinese dishes. Today most towns of any size have at least one Chinese grocery store or a market where such items as soy sauce, dried shrimps, canned bamboo shoots, water chestnuts, kanten, and the like are sold. It may be a little difficult to find some of the sauces and other preparations, but the owner of a Chinese restaurant will tell you where he gets his, or better still, may consent to sell you what you need. In the recipes given here substitutes for hard-to-get items have been suggested wherever possible.

Following are some of the sauces, seasonings, flavorings, garnishes, dried foods, and other ingredients which give Chinese
17 cooking its distinctive character.

SAUCES

As mentioned earlier, the Chinese take great pains to preserve or enhance natural flavors. Ingredients are prepared separately and some are seasoned before cooking, some during cooking, and some just before serving. In other words, it is not only the special sauces, herbs, spices, garnishes, and dried and pickled foods themselves which give the distinctive flavor, but also the care with which they are introduced.

Soy Sauce, a dark reddish-brown liquid, is made from salted and fermented soy beans. It is savory, rich in vitamins, and is as important to Chinese cooking as salt and pepper are to Western cooking. A glass container of soy sauce is a standard article on the Oriental table, and white mounds of rice drenched with the rich brown liquid are the Oriental counterpart of American potatoes and gravy. It is used to flavor and color sauces and gravies, as a marinade for ingredients before they are cooked, and as a dip sauce, either alone or in combination with other ingredients such as wine, vinegar, or mustard. While soy sauce itself is salty, it is not a substitute for salt.

Soy sauce comes in different shades and grades, as well as in different degrees of saltiness. Since it is so generally used in Chinese cooking it is important that a good grade be obtained. The quantity of soy sauce called for in each recipe is based on the strength of a good grade. If a cheap grade is used the quantity should be increased.

Oyster Sauce is a grayish brown liquid with a distinctive flavor. Many Westerners never acquire a taste for it. It is used to season rice gruel, steamed beef, and cold meats, especially cold chicken. It is somewhat expensive and more difficult to obtain than soy sauce.

Shrimp Sauce is another sauce for which one must acquire a taste. It is a greyish sauce with a strong shrimpy odor, used for cooking pork, sea foods, and vegetables.

Yu Loo is a strong-tasting fish extract.

Black Sauce (*Jee Yau*) is used to flavor fowl.

Fooh Yu is a sauce made of little cubes of pressed bean curd fermented in wine. White Fooh Yu, known as Soy Bean Cake comes in bottles and red Fooh Yu, known as Red Bean Curd comes in cans. It is used in cooking.

Dow See is fermented black beans.

Green Plum Sauce is used with any meat dish, just as Westerners use mango chutney.

Plum Sauce consists of fresh plum, garlic, red chili, sugar, salt, water, and alcohol, and corresponds to the Westerners' catsup.

Yennin Fruit Sauce is made of fresh yennin fruit, ginger, chili, sugar, and fruit coloring.

Hoisin is made of bean flour, garlic, chili, sugar, salt, ginger, spice, red beans, and water. It is used in cooking shellfish and duck.

Lemon Sauce is made of crushed lemons, sugar, wine, and water, and serves as a dip sauce for cooked meats.

SEASONINGS AND FLAVORINGS

Spices. The five spices most frequently used in Chinese cooking are fennel and Chinese anise, anise-pepper, clove, and cinnamon. A mixture of these is called "5-Spice," and can ·be bought at Chinese herb shops. The spices can also be obtained separately.

Ve tsin, or gourmet powder (monosodium glutamate), is a vegetable protein with little or no flavor of its own, which enhances the natural flavor of foods if added in small quantities.

Hua chiao mien-erh, or salt-and-pepper mixture, is made by heating 2 tablespoons of *hua chiao* (xanthoxylum) until it is brown and crisp, then rolling it to a fine powder and adding 1 teaspoon of salt. *Hua chiao* can be bought at Chinese herb shops.

Wine is used by the Chinese freely — in the kitchen to improve the flavor of the food and in the dining room to improve the flavor of the conversation and induce good fellowship. Sherry is specified in the recipes which follow since it is most like the yellow rice wine used in China.

Ginger is a tuber with a spicy flavor which finds its way— sliced, minced, crushed, or in the form of juice—into all kinds of dishes, meat and sweet alike. According to tradition, it has fountain-of-youth qualities, which may explain why it is so generally used. It is recorded that Confucius was never without ginger on his table. It should be peeled, and only fresh young roots should be used, as the flavor is more delicate and the root itself is less fibrous.

Garlic, minced, crushed, or in the form of juice, is a common ingredient used to flavor Chinese dishes.

GARNISHES

Lettuce. Crisp lettuce leaves are used to decorate platters or bowls of food. They look especially cool and fresh in combination with frothy white balls of deep-fried long rice.

Long Rice, or Bean Threads. This comes in long bundles. To prepare it as a garnish, break off the required amount, loosen it, and drop it into hot fat. It will puff up with an explosive crackling sound into a snow-white mass. Remove and let cool. Break into portions and use with crisp lettuce leaves to decorate a platter or bowl.

Nuts. Nuts are used as in Western cooking. Vegetable dishes are improved by garnishing them with cashew nuts, or with walnuts or almonds which have been shelled, blanched, peeled, and fried in deep fat until light brown.

Pickled Cucumbers may be used to garnish platters of meat or fowl. (See page 114 for recipe.)

Fruit. Pineapple tidbits and the white, translucent, fragrant lychee fruit are used to garnish meat dishes and desserts.

Sesame Seeds. These small, honey-colored seeds with a nut-like flavor may be sprinkled on almost any dish, from appetizer to dessert.

Parsley. Chinese parsley is quite different in appearance and taste from the stiff, frilly, dark-green parsley used in Western cooking. It is a lighter green, with a long willowy stem and flat leaves, and has a distinctive taste.

DRIED INGREDIENTS

Dried ingredients are as common in Chinese cooking as fresh frozen foods in Occidental cooking. This is partly because the Chinese feel that refrigeration destroys delicate flavors and food values and partly because facilities for freezing and packing are limited.

Down the center of many a Chinese grocery store are bins of dried ingredients, aromatic and, to Westerners, odd-looking, varying in appearance from hunks of dark brown leather to bundles of coarse grey hair or bunches of black steel wool. Many everyday recipes call for at least one or two of these dried ingredients, and anyone who is serious about Chinese cooking should become acquainted with them. It is true that canned mushrooms may be substituted for large dried Chinese mushrooms, but neither the taste nor the appearance is quite the same. More and more of these dried foods are being packaged in cellophane and sold in the larger grocery stores.

Dried ingredients are soaked in cold or lukewarm water until they have expanded sufficiently to be washed thoroughly and the unwanted parts can be cut away. They are then soaked in a second water until soft, after which they may be squeezed dry and prepared according to instructions. The second water is usually saved and either added to broth or used as a substitute for water if called for in the recipe.

Following are the dried ingredients called for in these recipes, and the time required to soak them.

Abalone. Soak in cold water 24 hours. Scrub thoroughly.

Bird's Nest. Soak ½ pound in 10 cups of water for 8 hours or overnight.

Cuttlefish. Cover with water, soak 20 minutes, and rinse well.

Fungi. Rinse well and soak 1 cup in 3 cups of warm water 30 minutes. Wash well.

Jelly Fish. Cover with water and soak 40 minutes.

Lily Buds. Cover with water and soak 20 minutes.

Lotus Seeds. Soak ½ cup in 2 cups hot water 45 minutes.

Mushrooms. Soak in warm water to cover until they expand. Wash well and remove stems and any foreign particles. Soak in second water until soft. Squeeze dry and prepare according to instructions.

Oysters. Soak in cold water until they expand. Wash thoroughly and soak in warm water 8 hours. Slit hard portion, clean out sand, and wash thoroughly.

Scallops. Rinse well, cover with water, and soak 45 minutes.

Shrimps. Rinse well, cover with water, and soak 20 minutes.

Squid. Cover with warm water and let stand 25 minutes. Wash thoroughly.

Shark fin. Wash thoroughly and soak in plenty of water 6 hours.

Seaweed. Rinse well and soak in warm water 25 minutes.

Preserved Turnips. Separate the turnips, rinse well, cover with water, and soak 45 minutes.

OTHER

Taofu, or bean curd, is a soft vegetable cheese which is inexpensive, highly nutritious, and easily digested. Made from soy bean milk, it has little flavor of its own and is usually eaten as an acompaniment to other foods or as an ingredient of highly flavored dishes. It may be eaten with soy sauce in its fresh state, added to soups, or cooked with meat, fish, or vegetable dishes. It may be cut in 1-inch squares, which are then slit, filled with wun tun filling, and deep fried. Or, cut into 1 x 2-inch slices and pan fried to a golden brown, it may be served plain with egg or meat dishes, or sprinkled with chopped green onions and covered with sweet-sour sauce.

Taofu comes in several different forms: (1) regular taofu, in blocks about 3 x 4 inches; (2) water taofu, which is like a thin custard; (3) pressed taofu, in cakes which have been pressed firm enough to be cut into any form desired; and (4) cakes which have been deep fried.

COOKING UTENSILS

厨
器
具

Although it is possible for the American housewife to cook most Chinese dishes without adding to her kitchen equipment, there are three or four items she may want to buy simply because they are efficient, versatile, economical of heat, and do not get out of order easily. She may even become attached to them and discard some of her more expensive equipment in their favor. The utensils mentioned below can be bought at any Chinese hardware store.

The wock, a natural outgrowth of the Chinese method of cooking, is a circular two-handled iron pan, shallow enough for pan frying, yet deep enough for fricasseeing and deep frying. Unlike the heavy frying pan found in most American kitchens, the wock is relatively thin. This and the rounded bottom permit the

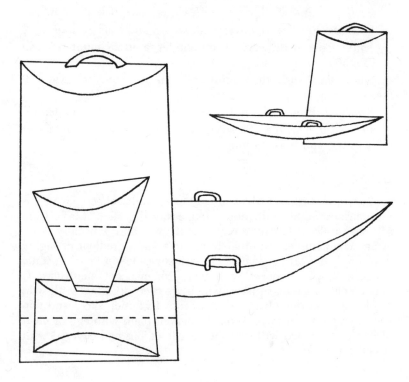

quick concentrated heat required for most Chinese cooking. The rounded bottom also does away with corners for food to get stuck in and burned, and makes stirring easier.

The wock, with a bamboo basket or a tier of bamboo baskets, suspended above it becomes a "wet" steamer, so called because the steam comes in direct contact with the article being cooked. Dumplings and buns are frequently cooked in this steamer.

Another kind of steamer requires a large pot with a cover and a small can or pot which has been perforated. Water is placed in the larger pot, the perforated pot is placed upside down in the bottom, and the container of food placed on top of it. The larger container is covered tightly, the water is brought to a boil, the heat is turned to medium, and as the water simmers the steam fills the pot and cooks the food. The steamer should be large enough to allow the food to be put in and taken out without burning the hands. The water should simmer gently and should reach about two-thirds up the sides of the bowl containing the food, neither high enough to boil over into the food nor low enough to boil dry before the food is done. The water level should never go below the half-way mark. Steaming time should be figured from the moment the water starts to boil.

A cleaver, or, preferably, a pair of cleavers, and a chopping block are needed to slice, chop, mince, dice, cube, and crush vegetables and meats. At first glance the cleaver may look rather formidable, but once the housewife becomes accustomed to using it she will find it her good friend.

Chopsticks are useful in the kitchen to stir, to pierce, to beat eggs, or to taste a dish before serving. The simplest way to get the drop of red in the center of a festive cookie is to touch it lightly with the tip end of a chopstick dipped in coloring.

CUSTOMS

用
膳
儀
式

The Chinese love of symbolism and play on words have led to interesting customs connected with food. To illustrate the play on words, the character for "onion" is one of two characters meaning "clever." In some parts of China, shortly after a child is born a tall man rubs a freshly cut onion over the baby's body. This is to express a wish that the child will be well formed and clever. In the case of chopsticks there is a double play on words. The characters for chopsticks, *faii jee*, mean "quick little boys," suggesting the speed and skill with which they set to work. Also, when a girl marries, her parents present her with ten pairs of red chopsticks, thereby expressing the hope that she will bring joy to the family by quickly producing little boys.

Important occasions call for certain dishes because of what they have come to signify. An American may wish his friend on his birthday "many happy returns of the day," but the Chinese accomplish the same thing by serving noodles (for long life) in a red basket (red is the color for joy). And the steamed buns, made in the shape of a peach, symbolize the magic peach of immortality which the God of Long Life eternally holds in his hand. In the case of a festival dish, it is well to follow the recipe as closely as possible — the omission of an ingredient may affect not only the taste but the reason for serving it at all.

Another interesting custom concerns the Kitchen God. In practically every home in China, pasted on the chimney or enshrined somewhere near the cooking stove, is the brightly colored picture of the God of the Kitchen. Since he presides over the activities of the kitchen, he is intimately acquainted with the events of the household and with the vices and virtues of each of its members. Once a year he ascends to Heaven where he makes a report to higher gods. His departure on the twenty-third day of the twelfth month and his return on the thirtieth are events of great importance and are surrounded with much ceremony.

On the night of the twenty-third, to the accompaniment of fireworks, prayers are said and incense is burned to the God of the Kitchen. His picture, faded and dusty now, is taken down and molasses or some other sweet, sticky substance is rubbed on his lips in the hope that his report to the higher gods will be influenced thereby. Sometimes, if the family is particularly apprehensive as to what the Kitchen God may report, his lips are rubbed with opium so he will be too drowsy to remember, or his picture is dipped in wine so that he will be intoxicated and the gods will refuse to listen to him.

The picture is then placed in a small chariot made of reeds or straw or mounted on a horse made of the same inflammable material, and transported with great ceremony to the courtyard or street where it can be safely ignited. With even greater ceremony the straw is set fire and the Kitchen God ascends in a cloud of smoke to present his annual report to the other gods.

A week of cleaning the kitchen and cooking the holiday dishes follows. On the night of the thirtieth the family gathers once more in the kitchen and with more firecrackers, incense, and prayers, celebrates the return of the Kitchen God. A bright new picture is enshrined, and promises and resolutions are made, which, if kept, will insure a glowing report for the coming year. In this atmosphere of hope and good will family quarrels are settled, friendships are renewed, and the new year is begun in a spirit of peace and happiness.

APPETIZERS

小品（引起食慾者）

Since the feast, rather than the cocktail party, is the principal social function in China, the Chinese have little need for cocktail *hors d'oeuvres* as Westerners know them. However, they do make savory bits of "small chow" called *deem sum*, which Western hostesses have discovered go well with drinks and add an exotic touch to any cocktail party.

The words *"deem sum"* mean "touch the heart," and the snacks coming under this designation are eaten between meals at odd times during the day, and even through the night, when a tasty morsel is craved and therefore most appreciated. They have become so popular for Chinese tea (from eleven in the morning to three in the afternoon) that some restaurants in the Orient serve only *deem sum* at midday.

Deem sum may consist of anything from raw seafood marinated in soy sauce and vinegar to steamed sweet pastry. Another kind of snack consists of dried and salted or spiced melon seeds, which are as popular in China as salted peanuts are in America. They are sold in shops and by peddlers on the streets and wherever people congregate, such as railway stations, public parks, theatres, and other places of amusement.

Deem sum may be either sweet, sour, or salty. The sweet ones go best with afternoon tea or at the end of the meal, and have been included in the section on Desserts. Those given here serve best as appetizers or cocktail fare.

ABALONE CUBES

紅
燒
鮑
寶

1 can abalone (16 ounces)   2 tablespoons sherry
1 cup soy sauce

Cook abalone according to either method described on page 50. Cut into ½-inch cubes, insert a toothpick in each, and arrange on plate. Serve with dip sauce made by combining the soy sauce and sherry.

CANTONESE SAUSAGES

臘
腸

½ pound Cantonese sausages

Wipe sausages thoroughly with a damp cloth and steam 30 minutes. Slice diagonally and arrange on plate or cut crosswise into thicker pieces and serve on toothpicks.

The sausages may be steamed in the usual way (page 23) or they may be buried in rice which is being steamed. The advantages of the latter are obvious—economy of time and fuel and the delightful flavor which the sausages give the rice.

CELERY AND SHRIMP EGGS

蝦
子
香
芹

1 pound celery stalks   1 tablespoon vinegar
1 teaspoon sugar   ½ teaspoon sesame oil
2 tablespoons soy sauce   1 tablespoon dried shrimp eggs

Cut celery stalks crosswise into 1-inch lengths and arrange on plate. Mix sugar, soy sauce, vinegar, and oil. Pour over celery, sprinkle with shrimp eggs, and serve.

Dried shredded shrimps may be used instead of shrimp eggs.

CRISP KAU TZE

紅
燒
餃
子

½ pound shrimps minced   2 teaspoons soy sauce
8 water chestnuts   ½ teaspoon gourmet powder
1 teaspoon fresh ginger juice Few grains pepper
¼ cup green onions, cut fine   30 wun tun doilies (see Crisp
1 teaspoon salt   Wun Tun Recipe, page 27)

Peel water chestnuts and mince. Combine shrimps, water chestnuts, ginger juice, and green onions, and mix well. Add salt, soy sauce, gourmet powder, and pepper. Spread doilies out on table and place a portion of filling in each doily. Moisten the edges with water. Fold over and press edges together. Deep fry until crisp.

CRISP WUN TUN

炸
雲
吞

Wun tun "skins" or "doilies" are thin 2½-inch squares of dough made with flour and eggs. They may be made at home or bought at a Chinese grocery store or restaurant. They are not expensive and unless you have unlimited time you will probably prefer to buy them. Filled with the following mixture and fried crisp in deep fat they may be served either as an appetizer or with the meal. The following recipe calls for 60 doilies.

FILLING

½ pound ground pork
8 water chestnuts
1 teaspoon fresh ginger juice
¼ cup green onions, cut fine

1 teaspoon salt
2 teaspoons soy sauce
½ teaspoon gourmet powder
Few grains pepper

Peel water chestnuts and mince. Combine pork, water chestnuts, ginger juice, and green onions, and mix well. Add salt, soy sauce, gourmet powder, and pepper. Spread doilies out on table and place a portion of filling in the center of each doily. Fold as shown below. Deep fry until crisp.

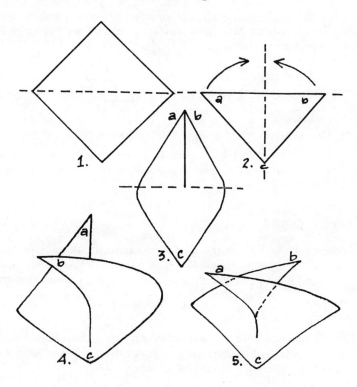

FRIED DUCK LIVERS

炸
鴨
肝

4 duck livers
2 tablespoons soy sauce
1 tablespoon sherry
2½ cups oil

½ teaspoon salt-and-pepper
   mixture (page 19)
MIX: ½ cup flour
   Pinch of baking powder
   ⅓ cup water

Cut each liver into 8 pieces and marinate in soy sauce and sherry 15 minutes. Add paste made of flour, baking powder, and water, and mix well. Heat oil and deep fry livers until light brown. Arrange on plate and sprinkle with salt-and-pepper mixture.

Chicken livers may be used instead of duck livers.

JELLYFISH AND CUCUMBERS

黃
瓜
炒
海
蜇

½ pound dried jellyfish
2 small cucumbers, shredded
5 tablespoons vinegar

1 tablespoon sugar
1 tablespoon sesame oil
1 tablespoon soy sauce

Wash jellyfish and scald with boiling water. Cut into strips 1 inch wide and slice each diagonally. Arrange jellyfish and cucumbers on plate. Mix vinegar, sugar, oil, and soy sauce. Pour over fish and cucumbers.

PINEAPPLE AND ORANGE BITS

波
蘿
橙
塊

2 slices pineapple
16 orange sections

1 cup oil
1 teaspoon sesame seed

Cut pineapple into bite-size wedges and arrange with orange sections on plate. Mix oil and sesame seed, pour over fruit, and serve.

LOTUS ROOT CHIPS

蓮
藕
片

Your guests will think these are extra special potato chips and will ask all kinds of questions, such as how you make them taste so good and what kind of cutter you use to get the fancy design.

2 lotus roots
2 cups oil

Salt to taste

Peel lotus roots and slice crosswise into very thin slices. Heat oil and deep fry lotus slices to a rich, golden brown. Drain on paper towel, sprinkle with salt, and serve.

PRESERVED EGGS

皮
蛋

Preserved eggs are the so-called ancient or thousand-year-old eggs sold in Chinese grocery stores. They are really only a few months old and have been preserved by a coating of lime, ashes and other materials. They should be washed thoroughly and the shells removed.

4 preserved eggs (p'i-tan)   2 tablespoons crushed fresh
4 tablespoons vinegar   ginger

Cut each egg into 6 pieces and arrange on plate. Mix vinegar and ginger and pour over eggs.

A favorite *hors d'oeuvre* at the American Embassy in Peking was a piece of *p'i-tan* and a piece of sweet pickle on a toothpick served with vinegar and ginger dip sauce.

SHRIMP CHIPS

蝦
片

1 pound fresh shrimps, minced   2¼ cups lotus flour
2 teaspoons salt   5 tablespoons water
1 teaspoon fish extract (Yu Loo) 2 cups oil
1 teaspoon gourmet powder

Add salt, fish extract, and gourmet powder to shrimps and mix well. Add flour and water alternately, a little at a time, until all is used. Knead well. Make into 4 rolls, each about 6 inches long and 1 inch in diameter. Put in a large bowl and steam 45 minutes. Let stand in a cool place overnight to dry out. Cut each roll crosswise into very thin slices, spread on cookie sheets, cover with cheesecloth, and dry in the sun 2 days. Store in airtight container.

As chips are needed, heat oil and deep fry the desired number. When they have puffed up twice their size but are still white remove with a sieve, drain, and serve.

SHRIMPS ON TOAST

蝦
多
士

½ pound fresh shrimps, minced   ½ teaspoon salt
12 water chestnuts   1 teaspoon sherry
1 egg white   8 slices bread
1 tablespoon soy sauce   2 cups oil

Peel water chestnuts and mince. Combine shrimps and water chestnuts and add unbeaten egg white, soy sauce, salt, and sherry. Cut bread into 1-inch squares and spread with shrimp mixture. Heat oil and deep fry bread squares, face down, until light

brown.

SLICED HAM

火
腿
塊

½ pound boiled ham   1 teaspoon soy sauce
1 tablespoon sesame oil

Have butcher slice ham very thin. Cut each slice into pieces
1 x 2 inches. Arrange on plate. Mix soy sauce and oil and pour
over ham.

TAOFU AND SHRIMP EGGS

蝦
子
豆
付

12 1-inch squares taofu   1 teaspoon sesame oil
2 tablespoons soy sauce   2 teaspoons dried shrimp eggs

Pour boiling water over taofu. Drain and arrange on plate.
Mix soy sauce and oil and pour over taofu. Sprinkle with shrimp
eggs and serve.
Dried shredded shrimps may be used instead of shrimp eggs.

SOUPS

湯   The Chinese do not serve salads, nor would they think of drinking ice water with their meals. Instead, they put a bowl of hot soup on the table with other dishes and each person takes what he wants. Since it is usually a clear soup with a few morsels of meat and plenty of vegetables, it provides a hot tasty liquid to "wash things down," plus the vegetables which the Westerner usually eats in a salad.

The hot liquid soup is a perfect medium in which to serve fresh and dried ingredients together. Back in the mists of antiquity the Chinese discovered that their vegetables eaten raw could spread disease. Cooked briefly they became safe and yet retained their color, taste, texture, and nutritive value.

The Chinese feel that refrigeration destroys food values and flavors, and their favorite method of preserving food is still the simple and ancient way of drying in the sun and wind. Dried foods, soaked until tender and then cooked briefly with the fresh vegetables are an important ingredient of soups.

Most Chinese soups are clear, not creamy, and may be prepared in a half hour or less. A few special delicacies, such as bird's nest or shark fin soup, take longer, however. Another type of soup or chowder is thicker and also takes longer to prepare. Chowders are included with the rice recipes.

Many soups are quasi-medicinal in nature and are eaten during pregnancy, after childbirth, during convalescence, or simply as an insurance against illness, much as vitamin capsules are taken in the West. A doctor's first recommendation usually concerns the patient's diet. If the patient does not improve, the doctor prescribes medicines in the form of food, such as tiger tendon and quince wine or a dark chicken-and-herb soup. Chinese medicines frequently have soups and stews concocted around them, making them more palatable than Occidental pills, draughts, and drugs.

Several of the recipes in this book call for water or stock. The latter should be used whenever possible for its added flavor and nourishment. The Chinese use bones, of course, in making stock, but the scarcity of food has taught them also to use many things which Westerners throw away, such as vegetable tops and peelings, pea and bean pods, and meat scraps. The liquid in which vegetables have been cooked, the liquor from canned products, even the water in which dried foods have been soaked is saved and added to soup or stock.

Three recipes for stock precede the soup recipes in this section. Pork or beef stock may be improved by the addition of shredded chicken, dried squid, scallops, shrimps, or other shellfish such as clams or lobster. Pork and chicken may be combined but not pork and beef. Stock, in contrast to the "quick soups," becomes more concentrated and delicious the longer it is cooked.

BEEF STOCK

牛
肉
上
湯

1 pound beef, shredded
7 cups cold water
1 tablespoon soy sauce

Salt to taste
1 teaspoon sesame oil

Bring beef and water to a boil and simmer 30 minutes. Add soy sauce, salt, and oil.

CHICKEN STOCK

鷄
肉
上
湯

1 fryer (3½ pounds)
½ pound pork, shredded
6 cups water
2 teaspoons soy sauce

Salt to taste
1 teaspoon gourmet powder
½ teaspoon sesame oil

Bring chicken, pork, and water to a boil and continue boiling 10 minutes. Simmer 40 minutes and remove chicken. Add soy sauce, salt, gourmet powder, and oil. Serves 5.

PORK STOCK

Follow the recipe for Beef Stock, substituting 1 pound of pork, shredded. If you have pork bones on hand add them during simmering.

ABALONE SOUP

鮑
魚
湯

1 can abalone (16 ounces),
    sliced
8 water chestnuts
1 can mushrooms (4 ounces)
1 can chicken broth (14 ounces)

6 cups water
¾ pound pork, sliced
1 teaspoon soy sauce
Salt to taste

Cook abalone according to either method described on page 50. Peel water chestnuts and slice. Bring abalone liquor, mushroom liquor, chicken broth, and water to a boil. Add water chestnuts, mushrooms, and pork. Simmer 15 minutes. Add abalone, soy sauce, and salt. Bring the soup once more to a boil. Serves 6.

BIRD'S NEST SOUP

燕
窩
湯

This famous soup dates back to the thirteenth century when Genghis Khan and his Mongol hordes invaded China. The Sung emperor, retreating from one city to the next, finally took refuge with his remaining followers on the tiny island of Yaishang. Unable to get food through the Mongol blockade, they were forced to live on anything they could find, even the nests of the swallows, which contained food the parent birds had stored for their young. Eventually the emperor gave up hope of retaining his throne and threw himself into the sea, to be followed by many of his court. Since then bird's nest soup has been served in memory of the fallen emperor.

Breast meat of 1 chicken
    (3 pounds)
2 teaspoons cornstarch
1 teaspoon salt
½ cup cold water
2 egg whites

½ pound white bird's nest
9 cups rich chicken stock
2 tablespoons chopped ham
2 tablespoons chopped parsley
Salt to taste

Prepare breast meat as in Chicken Velvet and Corn recipe (page 69). Soak bird's nest 1 hour in 9 cups water. Wash carefully several times, removing tiny feathers. Cover with 9 cups water, bring to a boil, and simmer ½ hour. Drain and repeat process. Drain. Add bird's nest to chicken stock, bring to a boil, and simmer 20 minutes. Remove from heat and add chicken velvet. Stir well and reheat. Add chopped ham, parsley, and salt. Serves 8.

Chicken velvet may be omitted but the soup will not be nearly so rich or tasty.

CELERY CABBAGE SOUP

紹
菜
湯

5 cups sliced celery cabbage
½ cup green onions, cut in
    1-inch lengths
¼ cup dried shrimps
3 cans (14-ounce size) chicken
    broth

⅓ cup ground pork
1 cup water
½ teaspoon gourmet powder
Salt to taste
1 tablespoon crushed fresh
    ginger

Mix all ingredients except celery cabbage, bring to a boil, and simmer 10 minutes. Add cabbage and simmer 15 minutes. Serves 4.

CELERY CABBAGE SOUP WITH PORK BALLS

肉
丸
紹
菜
湯

3 cups sliced celery cabbage
7 cups water
Bones of 1 chicken
Salt to taste

2 teaspoons soy sauce
1 tablespoon cornstarch
1 tablespoon sherry
½ pound ground pork

Bring water and chicken bones to a boil, add celery cabbage, and simmer 30 minutes. Remove bones. Add salt and soy sauce. Mix cornstarch and sherry and add to ground pork. Form pork into small balls and drop into soup. Simmer 15 minutes. Serves 4.

CHICKEN SOUP

鶏
湯

1 fryer (2½ pounds)
8 cups water
6 medium-sized dried
    mushrooms

1 bamboo shoot, shredded
¼ pound boiled ham, shredded
2 teaspoons soy sauce
Salt to taste

Bring chicken and water to a boil and continue boiling 6 minutes. Soak mushrooms and clean (page 21). Squeeze dry and shred. Add mushrooms and bamboo shoot to chicken and simmer 40 minutes. Remove chicken. Cut off breast meat and shred. Add shredded chicken and ham, soy sauce, and salt to soup. Simmer 20 minutes. Serves 6.

CHINESE OKRA SOUP

勝
瓜

¾ pound pork
6 cups water
¼ cup dried shrimps
1 tablespoon crushed fresh
    ginger

1 pound okra, sliced
½ cup green onions, cut in
    1-inch lengths
Salt to taste

湯　　　Bring pork and water to a boil. Add shrimps and ginger and simmer 20 minutes. Add okra and simmer 10 minutes. Remove meat and slice fine. Add meat to soup and reheat. Add onions and salt. Serves 5.

EGG FLOWER SOUP

蛋
花
湯

2 eggs	1 teaspoon soy sauce
2 cups chicken stock	Salt to taste

Beat eggs with fork until lemon-colored. Bring stock to a boil and add eggs, stirring constantly. Add soy sauce and salt. Serves 2.

FIG SOUP

無
花
菓
湯

4 figs	6 dried dates
¾ pound lean pork, sliced	6 cups water
1 slice ginger	Salt to taste

Wash figs and cut into halves. Wash dates. Bring pork, ginger, dates, and water to a boil and simmer 20 minutes. Add figs and simmer 15 minutes. Salt to taste. Serves 5.

LOTUS ROOT SOUP

蓮
藕
湯

2 cups sliced lotus root	6 cups water
½ pound beef, sliced	1 tablespoon soy sauce
6 dried dates (optional)	Salt to taste

Bring lotus root, beef, dates, and water to a boil. Simmer 30 minutes. Add soy sauce and salt. Serves 5.

A shin bone with meat on it may be substituted for the sliced beef and the soup cooked 15 minutes longer.

MUSHROOM SOUP

冬
菇
湯

12 medium-sized dried mushrooms	6 cups water
6 water chestnuts	1 bamboo shoot, sliced
½ pound pork, shredded	¼ pound boiled ham, shredded
	Salt to taste

Soak mushrooms and remove stems (page 21). Peel water chestnuts and slice. Bring pork and water to a boil and continue boiling 2 minutes. Add mushrooms, water chestnuts, and bamboo shoot. Simmer 30 minutes. Add ham and salt and simmer 5 minutes. Serves 5.

MUSTARD CABBAGE SOUP

芥
荣
湯

3 cups mustard cabbage stalks,
    cut in 1-inch lengths
½ pound pork, shredded
Bones of 1 chicken

7 cups water
2 teaspoons soy sauce
Salt to taste

Bring pork, chicken bones, and water to a boil and simmer 30 minutes. Remove bones. Add mustard cabbage and boil 2 minutes with pot uncovered so the vegetable will stay green. Add soy sauce and salt. Serves 6.

OXTAIL SOUP

牛
尾
湯

1 oxtail, cut in 2-inch pieces
¼ cup black beans
½ cup raw peanuts
2 tablespoons oil
2 tablespoons soy sauce

1 teaspoon salt
1 onion sliced
2 cups sliced carrots
2 cups sliced turnips
8 cups water

Wash beans and soak 2 hours in 1 cup water. Wash peanuts and soak 2 hours. Cover with water, bring to a boil, and continue boiling 5 minutes. Remove and shell. Wash oxtail well and remove excess fat. Bring to a boil in 3 cups water, simmer 5 minutes, and remove. Heat pan, add oil, and sauté oxtail 1 minute. Add soy sauce and salt. Combine oxtail, beans, peanuts, onion, carrots, and turnips. Add 8 cups of water, bring to a boil and simmer 2 hours. Remove oxtail and separate meat from bones. Return meat to soup and reheat. Serves 6.

PAPAYA SOUP

木
瓜
湯

1 pound green papaya
1 dried cuttlefish
Pork bones
¾ cup raw peanuts, shelled

1 slice fresh ginger
6 cups water
Salt to taste
1 teaspoon gourmet powder

Peel papaya and cut into 1-inch cubes. Rinse cuttlefish and soak 30 minutes in 2 cups warm water. Wash and remove shell. Bring cuttlefish, pork bones, raw peanuts, ginger, and water to a boil. Simmer 1½ hours. Add papaya and simmer ½ hour. Add salt and gourmet powder. Serves 4.

SHARK FIN SOUP

魚翅湯

6 ounces dried shark fin
¾ pound lean pork
Pork bones
8 cups water

1 fryer (2½ pounds)
Salt to taste
MIX: 2 teaspoons cornstarch
2 tablespoons water

Rinse shark fin and soak 4 hours in 8 cups warm water. Pour off water, rinse again, and drain. Place in a pot, add 6 cups warm water, bring to a boil, and simmer 1 hour. Pour off the water and repeat process. Drain.

Bring pork, pork bones, and 8 cups water to a boil and simmer 15 minutes. Add chicken and simmer 30 minutes. Remove chicken, pork, and pork bones. Remove breast meat of chicken and shred. Add shark fin to stock and simmer 1 hour. Add shredded breast meat, salt, and mixture of cornstarch and water. Simmer 5 minutes. Serves 6.

SPINACH AND FISH CAKE SOUP

波菜魚丸湯

½ bunch spinach, cut in
    1-inch lengths
½ pound fish cake
4 water chestnuts
1 tablespoon green onions, cut
    in ¼-inch lengths

½ pound pork
6 cups water
Salt to taste
1 teaspoon gourmet powder

Peel water chestnuts and mince. Combine fish cake, water chestnuts, and green onions. Mix well and form into 10 balls. Bring pork and water to a boil and simmer 15 minutes. Add spinach, fish-cake balls, gourmet powder, and salt. Bring to a boil and simmer 15 minutes.

SPINACH AND PORK BALL SOUP

肉丸波菜湯

½ bunch spinach, cut in
    1-inch lengths
3 cups cold water
½ pound ground pork

MIX: 2 tablespoons cornstarch
½ teaspoon salt
1 teaspoon sesame oil

Bring spinach and water to a boil and continue boiling 10 minutes. Add cornstarch, salt, and sesame oil mixture to pork. Form into small balls and drop into spinach soup. Simmer 15 minutes. Serves 3.

TAOFU, EGG, AND CHICKEN BLOOD SOUP

鶏
血
豆
付
蛋
湯

1 block taofu
2 eggs
4 tablespoons oil
1 cup chicken blood

3 cups water
1 teaspoon vinegar
1 teaspoon soy sauce
Pinch of pepper

Dip taofu into boiling water, remove, and cut into thin strips about 1 inch long. Beat eggs until lemon-colored. Heat pan, add oil, and fry one-half of beaten eggs in a thin omelet. Remove to plate and repeat process. Cut omelets into thin strips. Add chicken blood to boiling water and let simmer 1 minute. Remove coagulated blood to plate and cut into thin strips about 1 inch long. Bring 3 cups water to a boil, add shredded bean curd and chicken blood, and simmer 10 minutes. Add shredded eggs, vinegar, soy sauce, and pepper. Serves 4.

TAOFU, EGG, AND PORK SOUP

豆
腐
猪
肉
蛋
湯

1 block taofu
2 eggs
4 tablespoons oil
1 can chicken broth (14 ounces)
7 cups water

¾ pound pork, shredded
3 tablespoons vinegar
2 teaspoons soy sauce
1¼ teaspoons pepper
1 teaspoon salt

Dip taofu into boiling water, remove, and cut into thin strips about 1 inch long. Beat eggs until lemon-colored. Heat pan, add oil, and fry one-half of beaten eggs in a thin omelet. Remove to plate and repeat process. Cut omelets into thin strips. Bring the chicken broth and water to a boil, add taofu, eggs, pork, vinegar, salt, soy sauce, and pepper. Simmer 2 minutes. Serves 8.

TURKEY BONES AND CELERY CABBAGE SOUP

紹
菜
火
鶏
骨
湯

Turkey bones (from thighs,
    drumsticks, wings, and
    neck)
9 cups water
6 cups celery cabbage, cut in
    1-inch lengths

4 tablespoons dried shrimps
1 piece dried tangerine skin
1 small slice fresh ginger
Salt to taste

Bring turkey bones and water to boil and simmer 15 minutes. Add celery cabbage, shrimps, tangerine skin, and ginger. Simmer 30 minutes. Remove bones and add salt to taste. Serves 8.

The tangerine skin and ginger may be omitted if desired.

TURNIP AND PORK SOUP

蘿
蔔
猪
肉
湯

1 turnip, sliced
½ pound pork, sliced
Bones of 1 chicken

4 cups cold water
Salt to taste
1 tablespoon soy sauce

Bring turnip, pork, chicken bones, and water to a boil. Simmer 30 minutes and remove bones. Add salt and soy sauce. Serves 3.

Three cups of mustard cabbage may be substituted for the sliced turnip.

TURNIP AND TAOFU SOUP

蘿
蔔
豆
付
湯

1 turnip, shredded
1 block taofu, cubed
¾ pound pork, shredded
2 tablespoons dried shrimps

1 can chicken broth
  (14 ounces)
6 cups water
Salt to taste

Bring turnip, pork, shrimps, chicken broth, and water to a boil and simmer 30 minutes. Add taofu and simmer 5 minutes. Add salt to taste. Serves 6.

VEGETABLE SOUP I

瓜
菜
湯

Add any or a combination of any of the following vegetables to Beef Stock, Chicken, or Pork Stock (page 32) and simmer 10 minutes:

bamboo shoots, sliced
broccoli, sliced
celery, cut in 2-inch lengths
celery cabbage, sliced
cucumbers, peeled and sliced
lettuce, shredded

dried mushrooms, whole (after
  being soaked and cleaned)
peas, shelled
radishes, sliced
spinach, cut in 1-inch lengths
water chestnuts, sliced
watercress, cut in 1-inch lengths

VEGETABLE SOUP II

瓜
菜
湯

½ pound ground pork
6 small dried mushrooms
6 water chestnuts
1½ tablespoons salt
1 tablespoon cornstarch

4 cups water
2 bamboo shoots, sliced
24 Chinese peas
1 okra, peeled, sliced diagonally
1 tablespoon soy sauce

Soak mushrooms and clean (page 21). Peel water chestnuts and crush. Add water chestnuts, salt, and cornstarch to pork. Mix and form into 12 balls. Bring water to a boil, add pork balls, mushrooms, and bamboo shoots. Simmer 15 minutes. Add peas, okra, and soy sauce and simmer 10 minutes.

39

WATER CRESS SOUP

西
洋
菜
湯

¾ pound beef, sliced
4 cups water cress, cut in 2-inch
   lengths

6 cups water
1 egg
Salt to taste

Bring beef, water cress, and water to a boil and simmer 5 minutes. Beat egg with fork until lemon-colored. Stir into water cress and beef and simmer 25 minutes. Serves 5.

Six dried dates, a slice of fresh ginger, 1 dried cuttlefish, and 1 cup sliced taofu may be added if desired. Either pork soup or chicken soup may be substituted for beef and water.

EGGS

萓
類

The Chinese have found many appetizing ways of preparing eggs, but they do not serve them alone for their own sakes as generally as Occidentals do. Eggs combine with other ingredients and are often used to give definite form to soft foods or to bind others together, as in omelets and hash. Since they absorb flavors easily, they can be combined with meats, fish, shellfish, or fowl to give dishes with a high protein content, yet not requiring a large amount of meat. Egg strips, made by shredding omelets, are often used in soups or to garnish main dishes, as much because of their yellow color as for the nourishment they provide.

Everyone has heard of Chinese "thousand-year-old eggs," which are really only about 100 days old. The eggs are wrapped in clay made from ashes, tea, salt, and lime, and rolled in rice chaff so they can be easily handled. They are then buried under a few inches of earth and left 100 days. They are eaten without cooking and taste a little like cheese. The yolk is orange and the albumen is a dark green jelly with white flakes in it. Served with vinegar and fresh ginger they make a favorite appetizer.

Eggs are also preserved by a salting process (page 43). These eggs are popular, partly for reasons of color. After being cooked the albumen is still white, but the yolk has turned red—the color symbolizing joy.

The Chinese egg dishes most popular with Occidentals are of the omelet type. The omelets may be cooked large or small, folded or flat, and may be served with or without sauce.

Other dishes with eggs as an important ingredient but not given in this section include Egg Flower Soup (page 35) and several recipes for Pork Hash (pages 99–102).

CRAB OMELET (EGG FU YUNG)

蟹
蛋

6 eggs
1 cup flaked crab meat
1 tablespoon soy sauce
1 teaspoon salt
¼ teaspoon pepper

1 tablespoon cornstarch
Oil as directed
1 cup shredded bamboo shoot
½ cup shredded onions
½ cup shredded celery

Break eggs into large bowl. Add crab meat, soy sauce, salt, pepper, and cornstarch. Beat with egg beater ½ minute. Heat pan, add 2 tablespoons oil, and sauté vegetables 1 minute. Remove and let cool. Add vegetables to eggs and crab meat and mix well. Reheat pan, add 2 tablespoons oil, and fry in small omelets of two tablespoons each, adding oil as necessary.

SAUCE

2 teaspoons cornstarch
1 tablespoon soy sauce
1 tablespoon tomato catsup

1 teaspoon sherry
½ cup water

Combine ingredients and bring to a boil. Simmer until mixture thickens, stirring constantly. Pour over omelets and garnish with parsley. Serves 6.

EGGS AND WATER CHESTNUTS

荸
薺
蛋

5 eggs
14 water chestnuts
¾ cup fresh milk

⅛ teaspoon pepper
½ teaspoon salt

Beat eggs with fork until lemon-colored. Peel water chestnuts and chop. Add milk, pepper, and salt. Pour into medium casserole. Bake in moderate oven of 350° F. until set (about 50 minutes). Serves 3.

EGGS, SHRIMPS, AND VEGETABLES

蝦
蛋
炒
瓜
菜

5 eggs
11 tablespoons oil
½ cup sliced celery
1 cup sliced onions
¼ cup green onions, cut in
    ¼-inch lengths

¾ pound shrimps, sliced
1½ teaspoons soy sauce
¾ teaspoon salt
Few grains pepper

Beat eggs with fork until lemon-colored. Heat pan, add 3 tablespoons oil, and sauté vegetables 3 seconds. Remove. Reheat pan, add 2 tablespoons oil and sauté shrimps 2 minutes. Remove. Add vegetables, shrimps, soy sauce, salt, and pepper to eggs and mix well. Heat pan and add 3 tablespoons oil. Pour one half of mixture into pan, brown on both sides, and remove to serving plate. Repeat. Serves 4.

HAM OMELET

火
腿
蛋

½ pound boiled ham, shredded
5 eggs
12 water chestnuts
Oil as directed
½ cup sliced celery
½ cup sliced onion

½ cup sliced bamboo shoots
2 teaspoons soy sauce
1 teaspoon sugar
2 teaspoons salt
1 teaspoon pepper
1 tablespoon flour

Beat eggs with fork until lemon-colored. Peel water chestnuts and slice. Heat pan, add 3 tablespoons oil, and sauté vegetables 2 minutes. Add soy sauce, sugar, salt, and pepper. Remove to a plate to cool. Add flour to vegetables and mix well. Add vegetables to ham. Add eggs and mix well. Reheat pan, add 2 tablespoons oil, and fry in small omelets consisting of 2 tablespoons each, adding oil as necessary. Serves 5.

SALTED EGGS

咸
蛋

1 dozen eggs   *1 quart water*   *1½ cups rock salt*

Add salt to water and bring to a boil. Put eggs in a large jar. When water has cooled pour over eggs, cover, and let stand two weeks. Eggs are then ready for use.

To use: Cover eggs with cold water, bring to a boil, and simmer 16 minutes. Cool and shell. Cut each egg into six pieces.

Salted eggs are served for breakfast or after a nine-course dinner. Either duck or chicken eggs may be used.

BRAISED PIGEON EGGS

紅
燒
鴿
蛋

8 pigeon eggs, hard-boiled
1 small bamboo shoot, sliced
2 large dried mushrooms, sliced
⅓ cup flour
2 cups oil

MIX: *1 teaspoon cornstarch*
1 teaspoon sugar
1 tablespoon sherry
4 tablespoons soy sauce

Shell eggs and marinate in mixture of cornstarch, sugar, soy sauce, and sherry. Soak mushrooms, and remove stems (page 21). Squeeze dry and slice. Drop bamboo shoot and mushrooms in boiling water and parboil 1 minute. Remove. Rub each egg with flour. Heat pan, add oil, and fry eggs until brown. Remove and pour off oil. Reheat pan, add 3 tablespoons oil, and sauté bamboo shoots and mushrooms 4 seconds. Add marinade and eggs and simmer ½ minute. Serves 2.

SCRAMBLED EGGS AND SCALLOPS

干
貝
炒
鷄
蛋

4 eggs
½ cup dried scallops
1 teaspoon sherry

1 teaspoon soy sauce
½ teaspoon salt
5 tablespoons oil

Wash scallops and soak 2 hours in 1 cup cold water. Using the same water, bring to a boil and simmer, stirring constantly, until the scallops are well shredded and the water has evaporated. Remove scallops to a bowl and add sherry, soy sauce, salt, and 2 tablespoons oil. Heat pan, add 3 tablespoons oil, and sauté scallops 1 minute. Break eggs into a bowl, beat slightly, and add to scallops. Continue cooking until the eggs are scrambled. Serves 3.

SCRAMBLED EGGS AND SHRIMPS

蝦
蛋

6 eggs
½ pound shrimps, shelled and
   chopped
½ cup green onions, cut in
   ¼-inch lengths

½ teaspoon salt
2 teaspoons soy sauce
1 teaspoon sherry
4 tablespoons oil

Beat eggs with fork. Add onions, soy sauce, salt, and sherry to eggs. Heat pan, add oil, and sauté shrimps 2 minutes. Add egg mixture and cook over medium heat until set. Stir 1 minute until the entire mixture is cooked. Remove to bowl. Pour hot sauce over eggs. Serves 3.

SAUCE

1 tablespoon soy sauce
2 teaspoons cornstarch
1 tablespoon sherry

½ teaspoon sugar
½ cup water

Mix all ingredients and bring to a boil. Simmer 1 minute.

TEA EGGS

蛋
茶

6 eggs
1½ cups soy sauce

¾ cup water
⅓ cup black tea

Place unshelled eggs in pot with enough cold water to cover them. Bring to a boil and simmer 10 minutes. Remove eggs and place in bowl until cold. Remove shells. Bring soy sauce, water, and tea to a boil and simmer 2 minutes. Add eggs and simmer 4 minutes. When eggs are golden brown remove and serve.

SEA FOOD

海
鮮

The fish is held in high esteem by the Chinese. They admire its courage and the strength and purposefulness with which it swims upstream or against the tide. Since fish often swim in pairs they have come to symbolize conjugal happiness and family continuity. In Buddhism, the fish symbolizes freedom from earthly restraints. The practice of keeping goldfish in the house as pets originated in China. An old Peking saying, mocking the uniformity and lack of imagination in Peking dwellings, characterized them as "a mat covering overhead, an earthenware fish-jar, and a pomegranate tree."

An extensive coast line, swift rivers, and large lakes, as well as numerous streams, ponds, and pools, provide the Chinese with plenty of fish and shellfish, and the consumption of both is enormous. Most villages, if they lack natural pools, build artificial ones. Each body of water capable of sustaining marine life is stocked and fished by the family owning the fishing rights. There is no casual or sport fishing. Every fish, shrimp, or crab in inland waters belongs to someone, and trespassing on these rights is forbidden.

Millions of Chinese live on river boats, subsisting largely on the fish they catch. On the North China Sea men catch fish for sale with the aid of cormorants. The large birds are worked from rafts or boats, some tied by one leg, others tame enough to return with the catch. The cormorant dives for the fish and swallows it, but a tight ring at the base of the bird's neck prevents the fish from going any farther. The bird returns to the boat and the fisherman retrieves the catch for the market.

The Chinese have devised innumerable ways of preparing

fish, and, despite the lack of refrigeration, they are often served fresher in China than in the West. Most restaurants and stores keep their fish alive in great jars or tanks until they are ordered. Those brought in from the sea are either eaten at once or preserved by cooking, salting, or drying.

Through long practice Chinese cooks have learned to disguise the "fishy" taste of sea food by seasoning it with soy sauce, wine, ginger, and pickled vegetables, or combining it with other meats such as pork or chicken. Fish is frequently eaten raw with a soy sauce dip, a custom which Occidentals have been slow to adopt.

FISH

BLUE RIBBON OCEAN FILLETS

藍
海
帶
魚
塊

1 pound ocean perch fillets
3 tablespoons flour
½ teaspoon salt

1 teaspoon pepper
6 tablespoons oil

Cut fillets in 2-inch lengths. Cover with cold water and let stand 20 minutes. Drain. Rub with flour, salt, and pepper. Heat pan, add oil, and fry fish until brown. Remove to serving dish.

SWEET-SOUR SAUCE

1 tablespoon cornstarch
½ cup sugar
1 teaspoon soy sauce

½ cup vinegar
4 tablespoons water
¼ teaspoon Tobasco Sauce

Mix ingredients for sauce and bring to a boil. Continue boiling until sauce thickens, stirring constantly. Pour over fish. Serves 3.

CRISP FISH ROLLS

脆
魚
片

1½ cups fish cake
8 water chestnuts
4 large dried mushrooms
⅓ cup minced red roast pork
¼ cup green onions, cut in
    ¼-inch lengths
3 cups oil
¾ pound pork caul

MIX: ½ teaspoon sugar
⅛ teaspoon pepper
2 teaspoons soy sauce
2 teaspoons sherry
¼ cup water
1 egg, beaten
1½ cups bread crumbs

Peel water chestnuts and chop fine. Soak dried mushrooms and clean (page 21). Squeeze dry and mince. Place fish cake in bowl, add water chestnuts, pork, and green onions. Heat pan,

46

add 1 tablespoon oil, and sauté mushrooms ½ minute. Add mixture of sugar, pepper, soy sauce, sherry, and water and stir 2 minutes. Add mushrooms to fish cake mixture.

Cut pork caul into 3 pieces 8 x 11 inches each. Spread out the pieces of caul and place some of the mixture in the center of each piece, dividing it evenly. Fold top and bottom edges about 1 inch and roll. (Each roll will be about 6 inches long.) Dip each in beaten egg, then in bread crumbs. Heat oil and deep fry rolls until golden brown. Slice each roll diagonally. Serves 4.

FRIED FISH

煎
魚

1 mullet (1 pound)	1 small red pepper, chopped
MIX: 1 tablespoon cornstarch	MIX: 2 teaspoons cornstarch
1 teaspoon water	½ teaspoon salt
2 cups oil	2 tablespoons soy sauce
¼ pound ground pork	¼ cup stock
1 small onion, chopped	1 tablespoon sherry

Cut fish in two lengthwise and remove bones, head, and skin. Slash fish lengthwise and across (see below) and rub with mixture of cornstarch and water. Heat pan, add oil, and deep fry fish until brown. Remove and pour off oil. Reheat pan, add 2 tablespoons oil, and sauté pork, onion, and pepper ½ minute. Add mixture of cornstarch, salt, soy sauce, stock, and sherry. Bring to a boil and simmer 1½ minutes. Pour over fish. Serves 2.

Sole and bass also may be prepared in this manner.

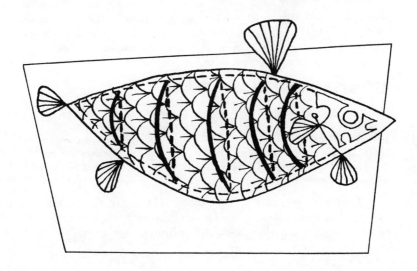

SLICED FISH AND CAULIFLOWER

魚
片
炒
菜
花

1 fish (1 pound), sliced
1 cup oil
1 cup cauliflower flowerets
1 cucumber, sliced diagonally
    very thin
½ cup water
½ teaspoon salt
1 teaspoon sugar

1 teaspoon soy sauce
1 teaspoon sherry
MIX: 1 tablespoon cornstarch
    ½ teaspoon salt
    1 teaspoon sherry
    1 teaspoon sesame oil
    1 egg white

Rub sliced fish with mixture of cornstarch, salt, sherry, sesame oil, and egg white. Drop cauliflower into boiling water and parboil 1 minute. Heat pan, add oil, and deep fry fish until it is light brown. Remove and pour off oil. Reheat pan, add 1 tablespoon oil, and sauté cauliflower and cucumbers 1 minute. Add water, salt, sugar, soy sauce, and sherry. Add fish, mix well, and cook 1 minute. Serves 5.

Sea bass is delicious served this way.

STEAMED FISH

蒸
魚

1 fish (1 pound)
3 dried mushrooms
2 tablespoons shredded ginger
2 tablespoons shredded green
    onions

MIX: 1 teaspoon cornstarch
    1 teaspoon sugar
    ½ teaspoon salt
    3 tablespoons soy sauce
    2 teaspoons sherry

Soak mushrooms and clean (page 21). Squeeze dry and shred. Clean fish and rub with mixture of cornstarch, sugar, salt, soy sauce, and sherry. Place on platter, garnish with shredded ginger, green onions, and mushrooms. Steam 20 minutes. Serves 4.

STEAMED FISH WITH BLACK BEANS

烏
豆
蒸
魚

1 fish (1 pound)
1 tablespoon oil
1 onion, sliced
1 tablespoon chopped ginger
1 tablespoon preserved Chinese
    black beans

1 button garlic, crushed
MIX: 1 teaspoon sugar
    1 teaspoon salt
    2 tablespoons sherry
    2 tablespoons soy sauce

Clean fish and rub with mixture of salt, sugar, sherry, and soy sauce. Place on deep plate. Cover fish with oil, onion, ginger, black beans, and garlic. Steam 20 minutes. Serves 2.

SWEET-SOUR FISH

甜
酸
魚

1 fish (1 pound)
3 cups oil
¾ cup shredded vegetables
    (onions, carrots, fresh
    ginger, and bell peppers)

MIX: 3 tablespoons cornstarch
      2 tablespoons water

Clean fish and make diagonal slashes on each side from tail to head (page 47). Rub with mixture of cornstarch and water. Heat pan, add oil, and holding the fish over the pan, baste the slashes with hot oil. Put the fish in the pan and fry until light brown. Remove to platter and pour off oil. Reheat pan, add 2 tablespoons oil, and fry vegetables 1 minute.

SWEET-SOUR SAUCE

1 tablespoon cornstarch
½ cup sugar
⅓ cup vinegar

6 tablespoons water
2 tablespoons oil
1 teaspoon soy sauce

Mix ingredients, bring to a boil, and continue boiling 1½ minutes. Add shredded vegetables and simmer ½ minute. Pour over fish. Serves 4.

Three-fourths cup of shredded Chinese pickles may be used instead of shredded vegetables. Red bell pepper adds a nice note of color. The golden fish should appear to be lying in a bed of brightly colored seaweed.

SHELLFISH

ABALONE

鮑
魚
類

3 dried abalones
1 chicken leg
½ pound pork
6 cups water

MIX: 1 teaspoon salt
      1 teaspoon cornstarch
      2 tablespoons soy sauce

Soak abalones 24 hours in 3 cups water. Scrub thoroughly. Cover with 4 cups water, bring to a boil, and simmer 45 minutes. Pour off the water. Cover abalone, chicken leg, and pork with 6 cups of water, bring to a boil, and simmer until abalone is tender. Remove abalone and slice. Remove chicken leg and pork. Add mixture of salt, cornstarch, and soy sauce to stock and cook until thickened. Pour over abalone. Serves 4.

ABALONE AND TRIPE

鮑
魚
及
牛
肚

1 can abalone (16 ounces)
10 water chestnuts
3 tablespoons oyster sauce
20 dried mushrooms
2 cups sliced bamboo shoots
1 pig's stomach
1½ teaspoons salt
½ cup lemon juice
4 tablespoons oil

2 cloves garlic, chopped
1 tablespoon chopped fresh
  ginger
2½ cups water
MIX: 2 teaspoons sugar
     2 teaspoons salt
     1 tablespoon soy sauce
     2 teaspoons sherry

Prepare abalone by either of the methods below, being sure to save the abalone liquor. Slice diagonally. Peel water chestnuts and slice. Soak mushrooms and clean (page 21). Combine oyster sauce and all but ¼ cup abalone liquor. Combine abalone, water chestnuts, and bamboo shoots. Add mixture of oyster sauce and abalone liquor.

Wash pig's stomach thoroughly, rub with salt, and let stand 5 minutes. Wash and scrape with spoon. Turn inside out and cut away excess fat. Wash, place in bowl, add lemon juice, and let stand 10 minutes. Rinse well with warm water. Drop into 5 cups of boiling water and simmer 10 minutes. Drain and repeat process. When cool cut into strips ½ by 1¼ inches.

Heat pan, add oil, and sauté garlic and ginger 3 seconds. Add pig's stomach and sauté 2 seconds. Add mixture of sugar, salt, soy sauce, and sherry, and sauté 1 minute. Add water and ¼ cup abalone liquor and simmer 5 minutes. Remove to a deep pot and simmer 1 hour. Add mushrooms and simmer ½ hour. Add abalone, water chestnuts, bamboo shoots, and oyster sauce. Simmer 6 minutes. Serves 6.

TO PREPARE ABALONE

Abalone comes fresh, canned, and dried. Unless cooked properly it becomes tough and rubbery. Canned abalone prepared in either of the following ways will be tender and will retain its color and sweetness. (1) Cover the unopened can of abalone with water and bring to a boil. Simmer 4 hours, being sure that the can is covered with water at all times. Remove, let cool, and open. Save the liquor. (2) Remove the abalones from the can and cut each in two. Put in a pressure cooker and add the abalone liquor and 1 cup water. Cook 20 minutes at 15 pounds pressure.

To slice abalone: cut in two lengthwise and slice diagonally.

ABALONE AND VEGETABLES

鮑
魚
及
菜

1 can abalone (16 ounces)
9 large dried mushrooms
3 water chestnuts
2 cups chicken stock
½ cup sliced bamboo shoot
1 tablespoon chopped onion
2 tablespoons crushed fresh
   ginger

½ cup abalone liquor
½ teaspoon salt
4 tablespoons soy sauce
1 teaspoon sherry
1 teaspoon sugar
MIX: 1 tablespoon cornstarch
   2 tablespoons water

Prepare abalone by either method described on page 50. Remove and slice diagonally. Save ½ cup abalone liquor. Soak mushrooms and remove stems (page 21). Squeeze dry and slice. Peel water chestnuts and slice. Bring chicken stock, mushrooms, water chestnuts, bamboo shoot, onion, and ginger to a boil and simmer until there is only 1 cup stock left. Add abalone liquor and simmer 1 minute. Add salt, soy sauce, sherry, and sugar. Bring to a boil and add abalone and mixture of cornstarch and water. Simmer 1 minute, stirring constantly. Serves 4.

A 4-ounce can of whole button mushrooms may be substituted for dried mushrooms and a package of frozen peas for the water chestnuts.

ABALONE, FUNGI, AND SUGAR PEAS

鮑
魚
木
耳
莞
豆

1 can abalone (16 ounces)
⅓ cup fungi
1 cup sugar peas

2 tablespoons soy sauce
½ teaspoon gourmet powder
1 cup water

Prepare abalone by pressure cooker method (page 50). Remove and slice diagonally. Soak fungi 20 minutes in 2 cups water. Wash thoroughly and drain. Add soy sauce and gourmet powder to liquid remaining in pressure cooker and bring to a boil. Add fungi and simmer 15 minutes. Add abalone and peas and simmer 1 minute. Serves 4.

STUFFED CLAMS

釀
蛤

15 medium-sized clams in
   shells
1 cup ground pork
1 teaspoon chopped ginger
⅓ cup chopped onion
3 tablespoons soy sauce

1 tablespoon sherry
¼ teaspoon salt
MIX: 1 teaspoon cornstarch
   ¼ teaspoon salt
   ¼ cup water

Wash clams, put in a saucepan, and cover with water. Bring to a boil and simmer 1 minute. Cool and remove meat, saving the empty shells. Chop clams and add pork, ginger, onion, soy sauce, sherry, and salt. Fill each shell with mixture and place on a deep plate. Steam 10 minutes. Pour mixture of cornstarch, salt, and water over clams and steam 10 minutes longer. Serves 2.

LOBSTER TAIL SAUTEED

炒
龍
蝦
尾

1 lobster tail (16 ounces)
4 tablespoons oil
2 cloves garlic, chopped
2 tablespoons crushed black
    beans
2 eggs
½ pound ground pork
¼ cup green onions, cut in
    ⅛-inch lengths

1 tablespoon chopped fresh
    ginger
¼ teaspoon gourmet powder
1 teaspoon sugar
3 tablespoons soy sauce
½ teaspoon salt
Few grains pepper
MIX: 2 teaspoons cornstarch
    ¾ cup water

Cut lobster tail crosswise, without removing shell, into 1½-inch pieces. Heat pan, add oil, and sauté garlic and black beans 2 seconds. Add lobster and sauté 2 minutes. Beat eggs with fork until lemon-colored. Add eggs, pork, green onions, ginger, gourmet powder, sugar, soy sauce, salt, and pepper to lobster. Stir ½ minute. Add mixture of cornstarch and water and simmer 1 minute. Serves 4.

LOBSTER TAIL STEAMED

蒸
龍
蝦
尾

1 lobster tail (16 ounces)
½ pound ground pork
2 eggs
2 tablespoons soy sauce
1 tablespoon sugar
1 teaspoon salt
1 tablespoon crushed black
    beans

3 cloves garlic, crushed
2 teaspoons crushed fresh ginger
¼ cup green onions, cut in
    ½-inch lengths
Few grains pepper
½ teaspoon gourmet powder
1 tablespoon oil

Cut lobster tail crosswise, without removing shell, into 1½-inch pieces. Place in a bowl shell side up. Sprinkle ground pork over the lobster. Beat eggs with fork until lemon-colored. Add rest of ingredients to eggs and pour over lobster. Steam 25 minutes. Serves 4.

One salted egg (page 43) instead of 2 fresh eggs may be used. It should be broken over the lobster after all other ingredients have been added.

LOBSTER TAIL WITH VEGETABLES

茶
炒
龍
蝦
尾

1 lobster tail (16 ounces)
4 tablespoons oil
2 cups cauliflower flowerets
1 can mushrooms (4 ounces)
1 cup sliced celery
½ cup cashew nuts

MIX: 1 teaspoon ginger juice
½ teaspoon garlic juice
2 tablespoons soy sauce
½ teaspoon sugar
½ teaspoon salt
MIX: 2 teaspoons cornstarch
½ cup cold water

Remove lobster meat from shell and cut crosswise into slices ½-inch thick. Soak in mixture of ginger juice, garlic juice, soy sauce, sugar, and salt. Parboil cauliflower (page 17). Heat pan, add 2 tablespoons oil, and sauté cauliflower, mushrooms, and celery 1 minute. Remove. Reheat pan, add 2 tablespoons oil, and sauté lobster ½ minute. Add cauliflower, mushrooms, and celery and stir ½ minute. Add mixture of cornstarch and water and stir 1 minute. Remove to platter and garnish with cashew nuts. Serves 4.

DRIED OYSTERS AND PORK

蠔
士
猪
肉

9 dried oysters
1¼ pounds belly pork
6 water chestnuts
2 tablespoons oil
2 buttons garlic

1 small onion, sliced
3 tablespoons soy sauce
2 tablespoons sherry
1 tablespoon sugar
2 cups water

Soak oysters until soft (page 21), saving ¼ cup of the second water. Cover pork with water, bring to a boil, and simmer 15 minutes. Remove and cut into pieces 1 x 2 inches. Peel water chestnuts; cut each into 4 slices. Heat pan, add oil, and fry garlic and onions until brown. Add pork and sauté 2 minutes. Add oysters, soy sauce, sherry, sugar, and oyster liquor. Cook 1 minute. Add water chestnuts and 2 cups water and simmer 30 minutes or until pork and oysters are tender. Serves 4.

DICED DRIED OYSTERS

蠔
士
鬆

12 dried oysters
8 dried mushrooms
1 tablespoon cornstarch
3 tablespoons water
½ cup ground pork
2 cups oil
1 bunch long rice
⅓ cup diced celery

⅓ cup diced onion
⅓ cup diced bamboo shoots
½ cup chicken stock
3 tablespoons soy sauce
1 tablespoon sugar
½ teaspoon salt
2 tablespoons sherry

53

Soak dried oysters until soft (page 21). Clean and dice. Soak mushrooms and remove stems (page 21). Squeeze dry and dice. Mix cornstarch and water and add to pork. Heat pan, add oil, and deep fry long rice until it puffs up and turns white. Remove and drain. Break into chunks and arrange on plate. Pour off oil and reheat pan. Add 2 tablespoons of oil and fry vegetables 1 minute. Add chicken stock and cook 1 minute. Remove to separate dish. Reheat pan, add 1 cup oil, and fry pork until well done. Pour off oil and reheat pan. Add 2 tablespoons oil and sauté oysters and pork ½ minute. Add soy sauce, sugar, salt, and sherry. Cook 1 minute. Add vegetables and cook 1 minute. Remove and pour over long rice. Serves 5.

STUFFED OYSTERS

釀
蠔
士

24 *dried oysters*	8 *water chestnuts*
2 *tablespoons soy sauce*	4 *cups oil*
3 *tablespoons sherry*	⅓ *cup chicken broth*
¾ *teaspoon salt*	¾ *pound pork caul*
2¾ *teaspoons sugar*	2 *cups bread crumbs*
¾ *pound ground pork*	2 *eggs, beaten*
⅓ *cup green onions, cut in*	
¼-*inch lengths*	

Soak dried oysters in 2 cups warm water 8 hours. Pour off the water. Slit the hard portion of each oyster and cut away the hard black substance inside. Rinse.

Mix 1 tablespoon soy sauce, 1 tablespoon sherry, ¾ teaspoon sugar, and add to pork. Peel water chestnuts and chop fine. Add green onions and water chestnuts to pork and mix well.

Heat pan, add 4 tablespoons oil, and sauté prepared oysters 2 minutes. Mix 1 tablespoon soy sauce, 2 tablespoons sherry, 2 teaspoons sugar, and ⅓ cup chicken broth. Add to oysters and stir until liquid has evaporated.

Cut pork caul into 24 pieces about 5 by 6 inches. Place an oyster on each piece of caul and put 1 teaspoon of pork mixture on each oyster. Fold in the edges of the caul and roll. Dip each rolled oyster in bread crumbs, then in egg, then in bread crumbs. Heat oil and deep fry oysters until medium brown. Serves 6.

Fish Cake may be substituted for pork.

STEAMED OYSTERS

Follow the above recipe, but steam the oysters 1 hour instead of deep frying them.

BRAISED PRAWNS

紅
燒
明
蝦

6 *prawns*
4 *tablespoons oil*
4 *tablespoons soy sauce*
1 *tablespoon sugar*
1½ *tablespoons sherry*

1 *tablespoon chopped fresh*
  ginger
1 *small onion, sliced*
1 *bamboo shoot, sliced*
¼ *cup water*

Remove legs but not shell from prawns. Heat pan, add oil, and fry prawns until they turn pink. Add soy sauce, sugar, and sherry. Sauté 2 minutes. Add ginger, onion, and bamboo shoot, and sauté ½ minute. Add water and simmer 1 minute. Serves 2.

Sliced cucumbers may be substituted for bamboo shoots and shrimps may be substituted for prawns.

PRAWNS AND ASPARAGUS

露
笋
明
蝦

4 *prawns*
2 *bunches fresh asparagus*
2 *tablespoons oil*
1 *teaspoon chopped fresh ginger*

2 *tablespoons soy sauce*
1 *teaspoon sugar*
1 *teaspoon sherry*
⅛ *teaspoon salt*

Clean prawns and slice crosswise into ¼-inch pieces. Clean asparagus and cut into 1-inch lengths, using only the tender part of the stalks. Bring to a boil in 2 cups of water and continue boiling 3 minutes. Drain, saving 2 tablespoons of the water. Heat pan, add 2 tablespoons oil, and sauté prawns until color changes. Add asparagus, ginger, soy sauce, sugar, sherry, salt, and 2 table-spoons asparagus water. Serves 2.

PRAWNS AND TAOFU

豆
付
明
蝦

4 *prawns, sliced*
3 *cups oil*
½ *block taofu*
1 *teaspoon sugar*
2 *tablespoons soy sauce*
1 *teaspoon sherry*
¼ *cup water*

MIX: 2 *tablespoons cornstarch*
½ *teaspoon salt*
2 *tablespoons soy sauce*
1 *teaspoon sherry*

Marinate prawns in mixture of cornstarch, salt, soy sauce, and sherry. Heat pan, add oil, and deep fry prawns. Remove and pour off oil. Cut taofu into 1-inch squares. Add sugar, soy sauce, sherry, and water. Simmer 1 minute. Add prawns and cook 1 minute. Serves 2.

PRAWNS AND VEGETABLES

菜
炒
明
蝦

4 prawns (boiled)
½ cup sliced carrots
2 tablespoons oil
1 stalk celery, sliced

¼ pound bean sprouts
2 tablespoons soy sauce
2 tablespoons sherry
¼ cup water

Clean prawns and cut crosswise into ½-inch pieces. Drop carrots into boiling water and parboil 1 minute. Heat pan, add oil, and sauté carrots and celery 1 minute. Add prawns, bean sprouts, soy sauce, sherry, and water. Cook 1 minute. Serves 3. Oyster sauce may be substituted for soy sauce.

SHRIMP BALLS

蝦
丸

1 pound shrimps, minced
10 water chestnuts
1 egg

4 tablespoons cornstarch
¾ teaspoon salt
1 teaspoon sherry
3 cups oil

Peel water chestnuts and mince. Combine shrimps and water chestnuts in a bowl. Beat egg slightly and add to shrimps and water chestnuts. Add cornstarch, salt, and sherry. Form into balls. Heat oil and deep fry shrimp balls until golden brown. Serves 4.

SHRIMP CROQUETTES

炸
蝦
圓

Follow the recipe for Shrimp Roll on page 57 but, instead of wrapping in pork caul, add white of 1 egg, mix well, and shape into croquettes about 3 by 1 inches. Dip croquettes in beaten egg, then in bread crumbs. Heat oil and deep fry croquettes until golden brown. Serves 4.

SHRIMP CROUTONS

麵
包
蝦
仁

1 pound shrimps
1 tablespoon cornstarch
1 tablespoon water
2 egg whites
12 water chestnuts
1 cup Chinese peas
2 cups oil

3 slices bread, cut into
    ½-inch cubes
3 tablespoons soy sauce
1 teaspoon sugar
½ teaspoon salt
2 tablespoons sherry
¼ cup water

Clean shrimps. Mix 1 tablespoon each of cornstarch and water and add to shrimps. Add egg whites and mix well. Let stand 10 minutes. Peel water chestnuts and cut into ½-inch cubes. Drop Chinese peas into boiling water and remove at once. Heat oil, and deep fry shrimps 2 minutes. Remove and drain. Reheat oil and deep fry bread until light brown. Remove to individual serving plates and pour off oil. Reheat pan, add 2 tablespoons oil, and sauté shrimps and water chestnuts 2 minutes. Add soy sauce, sugar, salt, and sherry and cook ½ minute. Add Chinese peas and ¼ cup water to shrimps and water chestnuts and cook 1 minute. Pour over bread squares. Serves 6.

SHRIMP ROLL

蝦
卷

1 pound shrimps
9 water chestnuts
¼ cup green onions, cut in
    ¼-inch lengths
1 teaspoon salt
2 teaspoons soy sauce

1 teaspoon sherry
¼ teaspoon pepper
4 cups oil
¾ pound pork. caul
1 egg, beaten
1¼ cups bread crumbs

Shell shrimps and clean. Wash 'well and mince. Peel water chestnuts and mince. Add water chestnuts, green onions, salt, soy sauce, sherry, pepper, and 2 teaspoons oil to shrimps. Mix well. Cut pork caul into three pieces 7 x 9 inches each. Place the shrimp mixture on the pieces of caul, dividing it equally. Fold both edges in about 1 inch and roll. Dip in beaten egg, then in bread crumbs. Heat oil and deep fry rolls until golden brown. Slice each roll diagonally. Serves 4.

SHRIMPS AND BROCCOLI

芥
蘭
蝦
球

½ pound shrimps
3½ cups broccoli flowerets
    and stems
6 tablespoons oil
6 tablespoons water

MIX: 1 teaspoon salt
2 teaspoons cornstarch
1 teaspoon sugar
3 tablespoons soy sauce
2 tablespoons tomato
    catsup

Clean shrimps, cut in two lengthwise, and cut each piece diagonally into three pieces. Marinate in mixture of salt, cornstarch, sugar, soy sauce, and catsup. Peel broccoli stems and slice diagonally. Heat pan, add 3 tablespoons oil, and sauté broccoli stems and flowerets 1 minute. Remove. Reheat pan, add 3 tablespoons oil, and sauté shrimps 2 minutes. Add broccoli and water. Mix well and cook 1 minute. Serves 3.

SHRIMPS, CELERY, PEAS, AND ONIONS

葱
豆
紹
菜
蝦

½ pound shrimps
5 tablespoons oil
1 cup diced celery
1 cup diced onions
½ cup frozen peas
6 tablespoons water

MIX: 1 teaspoon sugar
½ teaspoon salt
⅛ teaspoon pepper
2 cloves garlic, chopped
1 teaspoon fresh ginger
juice
2 tablespoons soy sauce

Clean shrimps and slice diagonally into pieces ½-inch thick. Marinate shrimps 30 minutes in mixture of sugar, salt, pepper, garlic, ginger juice, and soy sauce. Heat pan, add 2 tablespoons oil, and sauté celery and onions ½ minute. Remove. Reheat pan, add 3 tablespoons oil, and sauté shrimps 1 minute. Stir in peas, celery, and onions. Add water, mix well, and cook 2 minutes. Serves 4.

SHRIMPS AND CUCUMBERS

黄
瓜
蝦
球

¾ pound shrimps
3 cucumbers, sliced
  (not peeled)
3 tablespoons oil
2 tablespoons soy sauce
1 teaspoon sugar

MIX: 1 tablespoon cornstarch
½ teaspoon salt
1 tablespoon sherry

MIX: ½ teaspoon cornstarch
¼ cup water

Clean shrimps and rub with mixture of cornstarch, salt, and sherry. Heat pan, add 2 tablespoons oil, and sauté shrimps 1 minute. Remove. Reheat pan, add 1 tablespoon oil, and sauté cucumbers 2 minutes. Add soy sauce, sugar, and mixture of cornstarch and water. Simmer 1 minute. Add shrimps, mix well, and cook 1 minute. Serves 4.

SHRIMPS AND HEAD CABBAGE

椰
菜
蝦
球

¼ cup dried shrimps
4 cups sliced cabbage
½ teaspoon gourmet powder

½ teaspoon salt
½ teaspoon soy sauce

Bring dried shrimps to a boil in 2½ cups of water and simmer 10 minutes. Add cabbage, gourmet powder, salt, and soy sauce. Simmer 5 minutes. Serves 3.

A half pound fresh shrimps, cleaned and cut in two lengthwise may be substituted for dried shrimps.

SHRIMPS AND PEAS

青
豆
蝦
球

1 pound shrimps
2 teaspoons cornstarch
1 teaspoon water
1 cup oil
½ cup Chinese peas

MIX: 2 teaspoons cornstarch
1 teaspoon salt
2 teaspoons sherry
2 tablespoons water

Clean shrimps and rub with paste made by mixing 2 teaspoons cornstarch and 1 teaspoon water. Heat oil and deep fry shrimps. Remove and pour off oil. Reheat pan, add 3 tablespoons oil, and sauté peas ½ minute. Add mixture of cornstarch, salt, sherry, and water. Add shrimps and cook 1 minute. Serves 4.

SHRIMPS AND PINEAPPLE

波
蘿
蝦
球

1 pound shrimps
½ cup flour
½ teaspoon salt
2 eggs beaten slightly

3 pieces pineapple, cut into
½-inch pieces
3 cups oil

Remove shells from shrimps. Make a slit along the back of each shrimp ½ inch deep and remove black vein. Wash and drain. Add flour and salt to beaten eggs and beat well until it flows. Add shrimps to egg-and-flour mixture. Heat pan, add oil, and heat to 375° F. Add shrimps with some batter and deep fry until light brown. Remove and drain. Place on platter decorated with lettuce and fried long rice (pages 19-20).

SWEET-SOUR SAUCE

⅓ cup Heinz vinegar
4 tablespoons pineapple juice
2 teaspoons soy sauce

1 tablespoon cornstarch
½ cup sugar

Mix all ingredients. Bring to a boil and simmer one and one half minutes. Pour over fried shrimps and serve.

SHRIMPS AND VEGETABLES

茱
炒
蝦
球

1 pound shrimps
6 dried mushrooms
12 water chestnuts
4 tablespoons oil
2 celery stalks, sliced
2 medium-sized onions, sliced
¼ pound bean sprouts

MIX: ¼ teaspoon salt
1 tablespoon chopped
fresh ginger
2 tablespoons soy sauce
1 tablespoon sherry

MIX: 1 tablespoon cornstarch
½ cup water

Clean shrimps, cut in two lengthwise, and cut each half diagonally into three pieces. Marinate shrimps in mixture of salt, ginger, soy sauce, and sherry. Soak mushrooms and clean (page 21). Squeeze dry and slice. Peel water chestnuts and slice. Heat pan, add oil, and sauté shrimps 2 minutes. Add mushrooms, celery, water chestnuts, and onions, and cook 1 minute. Add bean sprouts and mixture of cornstarch and water. Stir 1 minute. Serves 3.

Chinese peas may be substituted for bean sprouts.

SQUID WITH BEAN SPROUTS

芽
菜
鮮
鰞
魚

1 pound fresh squid
4 tablespoons oil
2 cloves garlic, crushed
2 tablespoons crushed ginger
4 cups bean sprouts
½ cup water

MIX: 1 teaspoon cornstarch
1 teaspoon sugar
½ teaspoon salt
3 tablespoons soy sauce
1 tablespoon sherry

Wash squid, split down center, remove viscera and thin membrane, and clean thoroughly. Slash the inside diagonally crosswise and lengthwise, being careful not to cut through. Cut in two and then diagonally into 1-inch thick pieces. Heat pan, add 2 tablespoons oil, and sauté squid 1 minute. Remove. Reheat pan, add 2 tablespoons oil, and sauté garlic and ginger ½ minute. Add mixture of cornstarch, sugar, salt, soy sauce, and sherry and stir well. Add squid, bean sprouts, and water and cook 1½ minutes. Serves 3.

FOWL

鶏
類

The Chinese probably eat more chicken than any other nation. The chicken dish is considered the supreme delicacy, and the cook strives to achieve the ultimate.

Duck is also a favorite, and some of the Chinese duck dishes are world famous. Whole roasted ducks, brown and glistening, are a common sight hanging in Chinese meat shops. They may be taken home, heated, cut up, and served. At New Year's salted dried ducks are offered for sale. These flat and wizened little fowls are bought for flavoring. They are stored or hung in a convienient place so that from time to time small bits may be cut off and dropped into a pot of boiling rice or soup.

Small birds are seasonal delicacies in southern China. Quail and pigeon appear in the markets in early spring, and rice birds in autumn. To catch a sparrow or other small bird, the hunter dips the end of a long bamboo pole in birdlime, then stealthily insinuates the pole up through the branches of a tree, and slaps it against the bird. The lime holds the fluttering bird fast until the hunter puts it safely in the bag.

In old Peking a ten-day sale of fresh fowl marked the end of winter. Buyers thronged the northeast part of the city, and shouts reverberated through the crowded streets as sellers cried their wares from chicken and duck houses. Much more than a mere commercial event, this was an annual celebration. Not only did the young birds promise treats for winter-jaded palates, they heralded the renewal of life with the return of spring.

Many tales and beliefs have grown up around the fowl. The rooster, for instance, is considered to be the incarnation of *yang*, the male or positive principle of life. His crowing at dawn chases the ghosts of night away, the spurs on his legs indicate his warlike courage, and for some reason his crest symbolizes the literary spirit. Chinese New Year is the sacred day of the chicken and all Chinese observe it by at least a partial fast.

A pair of ducks is a symbol of conjugal fidelity; the dove is a symbol of many things, including faithfulness, long life, justice, and filial piety; and the pigeon is reputed to be the wisest of birds. Not long ago pigeons were still used by bankers and brokers to carry messages to their clients.

Raising pigeons used to be a popular hobby of mandarins of Peking. Special little whistles, made of the thinnest possible scraped bamboo and containing infinitesimal nuts and seeds to cause a trill, were attached just above the bird's tail. Most were single- or double-note whistles, but some had as many as nine, eleven, or thirteen pipes. When the pigeons wheeled overhead the music rose to the clouds, giving, we are told, "joy and a release to the emotions."

The Chinese use all parts of the fowl — tongue and coxcomb, liver and gizzard, wings and feet, and the skin is considered one of the most important parts. Even the heads and feet of small birds are used to decorate a dish. Westerners usually serve chicken disjointed or sliced but the Chinese frequently chop the fowl into small segments, using a cleaver to cut through the bones.

To cut a chicken into segments and arrange on platter:

Disjoint the chicken in the usual manner by cutting off the neck, removing the wings and legs at the joints, and cutting the body cavity into three pieces — the breast, the upper back, and the lower back. Cut off the lower, bony part of each drumstick. Using a sharp cleaver and cutting through the bones, divide the neck into 3 pieces, each wing at the joints into 3 pieces, each thigh into 2 pieces, each drumstick into 2 pieces, and the upper and lower back into 3 pieces each. Cut the breast in two lengthwise, then cut each half crosswise into 1-inch pieces. Garnish the platter with crisp lettuce leaves or long rice (page 19). Arrange the chicken in a neat pile, using the bony portions as foundation and ending with the pieces of breast meat.

To test a fowl for age:

The skin of a young chicken is smooth and the bones flexible. White skin is preferable, unless a fat bird is desired, in which case the skin should be moist and yellow. If the windpipe is soft and pliable, the bird is young; if it feels stiff and cracks when pinched, the bird is sure to be old and tough.

CHICKEN

BOILED CHICKEN

白
切
鷄

1 fryer (3½ pounds)
4 cups water
1½ teaspoons salt

2 tablespoons soy sauce
1 teaspoon sesame oil

Bring water to a boil and add salt. Add chicken and simmer 30 minutes. Remove chicken and let cool. Cut in segments and arrange on platter (page 62). Pour one of the following sauces over it and serve: Oyster Sauce, ½ cup; Plum Sauce, ¼ cup; Soy Sauce, 2 tablespoons to which 1 teaspoon sesame oil has been added. Serves 6.

BOILED CHICKEN WITH HAM

火
腿
白
切
鷄

1 fryer (3½ pounds)
4 cups water
16 thin pieces ham,
  2 x 1½ inches

2 tablespoons soy sauce
1 teaspoon sesame oil

Prepare Boiled Chicken as above, but instead of cutting into segments, cut meat into thin slices about 2 x 1½ inches. Arrange alternate slices of chicken and ham on platter. Combine soy sauce and sesame oil and pour over chicken. Serves 6.

CHESTNUT CHICKEN

栗
子
鷄

1 fryer (3 pounds)
4 dried mushrooms
24 chestnuts
4 tablespoons oil
1 large onion, sliced
1 tablespoon chopped
  fresh ginger

4 tablespoons soy sauce
1 teaspoon salt
1 tablespoon sugar
1 tablespoon sherry
1 tablespoon cornstarch
3 cups cold water

Clean chicken and cut into 2-inch segments (page 62). Soak mushrooms and clean (page 21). Shell chestnuts and blanch. Heat pan, add oil, and fry onion until light brown. Add chicken, mushrooms, and ginger, and sauté 2 minutes. Add soy sauce, salt, sugar, sherry, and cornstarch mixed with 1 teaspoon water. Sauté until brown. Add water and chestnuts and simmer until chestnuts are tender. Serves 6.

CHICKEN AND DRIED GOLDEN LILY BUDS

花
子
鷄

1 fryer (3 pounds)
½ cup dried golden lily buds
¼ cup fungi
½ cup dried mushrooms
1 cup sliced bamboo shoot
1 cup oil
2 cups water

MIX: 4 tablespoons soy sauce
1 tablespoon garlic juice
1 tablespoon ginger juice
2 teaspoons sugar
1 teaspoon salt
3 tablespoons sherry

Place chicken on platter and rub with mixture of soy sauce, garlic juice, ginger juice, sugar, salt, and sherry. Let stand 20 minutes. Wash dried lily buds, fungi, and mushrooms, and soak separately (page 21).

Heat pan, add oil, and fry whole chicken until brown. (Save whatever is left of the soy sauce mixture.) Remove chicken and pour off oil. Reheat pan and add 4 tablespoons of oil. Add lily buds, fungi, mushrooms, bamboo shoot, soy sauce mixture, and water. Simmer 2 minutes. Pour into deep pot, place chicken on vegetables, and cover. Bring to a boil and simmer 25 minutes. Remove chicken and let cool. Cut into segments and arrange on platter (page 62). Pour hot sauce over chicken. Serves 6.

CHICKEN AND GINGER ROOTS

子
羌
鷄

1 young chicken (1½ pounds)
½ cup sliced young ginger roots
3 tablespoons oil
1 small onion, sliced

2 tablespoons Hoisin Sauce
1 tablespoon soy sauce
1 teaspoon sugar
1 tablespoon water

Cut chicken into 2-inch segments (page 62). Heat pan and add oil. Add chicken and fry until brown. Add ginger roots, onion, Hoisin Sauce, soy sauce, sugar, and water. Sauté 1 minute. Serves 2.

Breast meat may be used instead of whole chicken; 3 tablespoons soy sauce may be used instead of Hoisin Sauce.

CHICKEN AND MUSHROOMS

冬
菇
鷄

Breast meat of 2 fryers
2 chicken thighs
6 chicken wings
1 8-ounce can whole mushrooms
1 cup water
¼ cup oil

MIX: 4 tablespoons soy sauce
3 tablespoons sherry
1 teaspoon salt
2 teaspoons sugar
2 cloves garlic,
chopped fine
2 tablespoons crushed
fresh ginger

Cut each breast and thigh into 3 segments and each wing into 2 segments. Marinate 45 minutes in mixture of soy sauce, sherry, salt, sugar, garlic, and ginger. Heat pan, add oil, and sauté chicken 5 minutes. Add water and mushrooms and simmer 25 minutes. Serves 4.

CHICKEN AND PEPPERS I

辣
菽
鶏

2 *chicken drumsticks*
2 *chicken thighs*
2 *cups cubed bell peppers*
8 *water chestnuts*
1½ *cups oil*
1 *cup cubed onions*

MIX: 1 *tablespoon cornstarch*
¾ *teaspoon salt*
2 *teaspoons soy sauce*
1 *tablespoon sherry*

MIX: 2 *teaspoons cornstarch*
2 *tablespoons soy sauce*
1 *tablespoon sherry*
¾ *cup chicken stock*

Remove meat from bones, and cut into cubes. Marinate in mixture of cornstarch, salt, soy sauce, and sherry. Peel water chestnuts and cut into cubes. Heat pan, add oil, and fry chicken 1 minute. Add peppers, onions, and water chestnuts and sauté 4 seconds. Remove and drain. Reheat pan and add 2 tablespoons oil. Add cornstarch, soy sauce, sherry, and stock mixture. Bring to a boil, add chicken and vegetables, and simmer 1 minute. Serves 4.

If one of the peppers is red it will add a pretty note of color to the dish.

CHICKEN AND PEPPERS II

辣
菽
鶏

This colorful dish, with its green, red, and white vegetables, is a favorite in Szechuen. The peppers should be hot. If they are not hot enough, dice 2 chili peppers and add to the vegetables.

2 *chicken thighs*
2 *chicken drumsticks*
1½ *cups oil*
1 *cup cubed red bell pepper*
1 *cup cubed green bell pepper*
1 *cup cubed onion*
8 *dried water chestnuts*

MIX: 1 *tablespoon cornstarch*
1 *tablespoon sherry*
¾ *teaspoon salt*
2 *teaspoons soy sauce*

Remove meat from bones and cut into cubes. Simmer chicken bones 6 minutes in 1½ cups water to provide stock for Sauce. Marinate chicken in mixture of cornstarch, sherry, salt, and soy sauce. Soak water chestnuts (page 21) and cube. Heat pan, add oil, and sauté chicken 1 minute. Add vegetables and stir 1 minute. Remove.

SAUCE

2 tablespoons oil
2 teaspoons cornstarch
2 tablespoons soy sauce

1 tablespoon sherry
¾ cup chicken stock

Heat pan and add 2 tablespoons oil. Mix ingredients and add. Bring to a boil, stir in chicken and vegetables and simmer 1 minute. Serves 2.

CHICKEN AND PICKLED VEGETABLES

酸
菜
炒
鷄

1 young chicken (1½ pounds)
½ cup oil
½ cup Chinese pickled
   vegetables (canned)

MIX: 1 tablespoon cornstarch
1 tablespoon soy sauce
1 teaspoon sherry

Cut chicken into 2-inch segments (page 62). Marinate in mixture of cornstarch, soy sauce, and sherry. Heat pan, add oil, and fry chicken until brown. Remove chicken and pour off oil.

SWEET-SOUR SAUCE

3 tablespoons oil
1 onion, sliced
2 tablespoons sugar
¼ teaspoon salt
½ cup pickled vegetable juice

½ cup chicken stock
1 tablespoon soy sauce
2 teaspoons sherry
4 tablespoons vinegar

Heat pan, add 3 tablespoons oil, and fry onion 3 seconds. Mix other ingredients and add to onion. Bring to a boil, add pickled vegetables and chicken, and heat through. Serves 3.

CHICKEN AND SLICED VEGETABLES

菜
炒
鷄

1 cup shredded breast meat of
   chicken
2 medium-sized cucumbers
1½ cups Chinese peas
1 cup sliced bamboo shoot
   (canned)

1½ cups chicken stock
1 cup oil
1 teaspoon salt
MIX: 1 tablespoon cornstarch
1 tablespoon water

Cut cucumbers lengthwise but do not peel. Remove seeds and slice fine. Heat pan and add oil. When oil is hot, add chicken and fry 1 minute. Remove chicken and pour off oil. Reheat pan, add 2 tablespoons oil, and sauté vegetables ½ minute. Add chicken and sauté 1 minute. Add stock and simmer 1 minute. Add salt and mixture of cornstarch and water. Simmer 1 minute. Serves 4.

Shredded celery (1½ cups) may be substituted for Chinese

peas.

CHICKEN CURRY

架
厘
鷄

1 fryer (3 pounds)
4 tablespoons oil
2 large onions, sliced
1 green onion, in 2-inch lengths
2 tablespoons soy sauce
2 red chili peppers (optional)
2 tablespoons sugar

3 tablespoons curry
½ teaspoon salt
6 small bay leaves
4 tablespoons shredded coconut
  (fresh or dried)
¼ cup coconut milk
2 cups water

Clean chicken and cut into 2-inch segments (page 62). Heat pan, add oil and sauté chicken, onions and onion tops ½ minute. Add soy sauce, chili peppers, sugar, curry, and salt. Sauté 1 minute. Add bay leaves, coconut, coconut milk, and water. Mix well, cover, and cook slowly until chicken is tender. Serves 4.

CHICKEN GIZZARDS

炒
鷄
腎

5 chicken gizzards
6 water chestnuts
2 tablespoons oil
¼ cup sliced onions
1 teaspoon chopped ginger
½ teaspoon salt

2 teaspoons sherry
2 tablespoons soy sauce
1 teaspoon 5-spice
1 large bamboo shoot, sliced
1 cup water

Remove fat and membranes from gizzards and cut open to remove inner sack. Wash and cut gizzard into 6 pieces. Peel water chestnuts, wash, and cut each into 6 pieces. Heat pan, add oil, and sauté onions, ginger, and sliced gizzards 2 minutes. Add salt, sherry, soy sauce, and 5-spice. Sauté 5 seconds. Add chestnuts, bamboo shoot, and water. Simmer 30 minutes. Serves 4.

CHICKEN ROLLS

鷄
卷

24 pieces of breast meat
    2 x 3 inches
12 pieces pork caul 5 x 6 inches
6 dried mushrooms
4 water chestnuts
1 large bamboo shoot (canned)
2 egg yolks

2 cups bread crumbs
4 cups oil

MIX: 2 teaspoons cornstarch
     ¾ teaspoon salt
     2 egg whites
     3 tablespoons soy sauce
     2 teaspoons sherry

Soak mushrooms and clean (page 21). Peel chestnuts. Chop mushrooms, chestnuts, and bamboo shoot. Put in a bowl and add mixture of cornstarch, salt, egg whites, soy sauce, and sherry. Put 1 teaspoon of mixture on each strip of pork caul and cover with 2 pieces of chicken. Turn up the edges of the pork caul about 1 inch and roll. Dip each roll in beaten egg yolks and then in bread crumbs. Heat oil and deep fry rolls. Serves 4.

CHICKEN VELVET

芙
蓉
鷄
片

This is a favorite Szechuen dish.

1 fryer (3 pounds)
1 tablespoon water (if needed)
2 teaspoons cornstarch
1 teaspoon salt
10 egg whites
½ cup water
¾ cup lard

MIX: 1 teaspoon salt
1 tablespoon cornstarch
¾ cup rich chicken stock
1 teaspoon sherry

Cut off the breast meat. Put the rest of the chicken, including the bones, in 3 cups water and simmer until a rich stock results. Pound the breast meat with the back of a Chinese cleaver or hammer 15 minutes, removing all the tendons while pounding. If meat becomes too dry add 1 tablespoon water and pound 15 minutes longer. Add dry cornstarch, salt, and 2 unbeaten egg whites. Mix well and add very slowly ½ cup cold water using 2 pairs of chopsticks, or a fork, or a wire whisk. Do not add the water too quickly or the mixture will not hold together. Beat remaining 8 egg whites until stiff but not dry. Carefully fold the chicken mixture into the egg whites. Heat pan and add lard. When lard is melted (but not too hot) pour in the mixture. Remove pan from fire at once and beat rapidly. After the lard is beaten into the mixture, replace on low heat and cook 4 seconds. Remove and pour through a strainer. Allow lard to drain. Reheat pan and add 2 tablespoons lard. Add mixture of cornstarch, salt, stock, and sherry and bring to a boil, stirring constantly. Add cooked chicken mixture, and heat through. Serves 6.

CHICKEN VELVET AND CAULIFLOWER

鷄
茸
椰
菜
花

1 fryer (3½ pounds)
1½ cups cauliflour flowerets
2 teaspoons cornstarch
1 teaspoon salt
2 egg whites
½ cup cold water

MIX: 3 cups chicken stock
1 tablespoon cornstarch
1 teaspoon salt
½ teaspoon sugar
½ teaspoon sesame oil
1 teaspoon sherry

Prepare chicken as in Chicken Velvet recipe to the point where ½ cup of water has been added slowly. Drop cauliflower in boiling water and parboil 1½ minutes. Bring mixture of stock, cornstarch, salt, sugar, oil, and sherry to a boil. Add cauliflower and simmer 2 minutes. Remove from heat and stir in chicken velvet. Reheat 1 minute and serve at once. Serves 4.

CHICKEN VELVET AND CORN

鶏
茸
粟
米

1 fryer (3½ pounds)
1 can creamed corn
   (17 ounces)
2 teaspoons cornstarch
1 teaspoon salt

2 egg whites
½ cup water
2 tablespoons oil
2½ cups chicken stock

Prepare chicken as in Chicken Velvet recipe to the point where ½ cup water has been added slowly. Heat pan and add oil. Add corn and chicken stock. Bring to a boil, add chicken, and stir 1 minute. Serves 6.

CHICKEN WINGS, PEKING STYLE

北
平
鶏
翼

1 pound chicken wings
1 tablespoon crushed fresh
   ginger
1 small chili pepper (fresh)
4 tablespoons sugar
½ cup soy sauce
1 star anise

2 teaspoons 5-Spice
2 teaspoons cornstarch
½ cup water
2 tablespoons sherry
1 tablespoon oil
4 hard-boiled eggs, shelled

Mix all ingredients together, except chicken wings and eggs. Bring to a boil. Add chicken wings and simmer 15 minutes. Add eggs (whole) and simmer 20 minutes. Serves 4.

FRIED CHICKEN

炸
子
鶏

1 fryer (3½ pounds)
½ cup soy sauce
1 teaspoon salt
1 tablespoon sherry
2 teaspoons sugar
2 cloves garlic, chopped

2 tablespoons chopped fresh
   ginger
2 eggs, beaten
2 cups bread crumbs
3 cups oil

Disjoint the chicken and put pieces in a large bowl. Combine soy sauce, salt, sherry, sugar, garlic, and ginger. Pour over chicken and let stand 30 minutes. Dip each piece of marinated chicken in beaten eggs, then in bread crumbs. Heat oil to 380° F. and deep fry chicken until brown. Cut chicken for serving and arrange on platter (page 62). Serves 4.

Chicken may be fried without the coating of egg and bread crumbs if desired.

CHINESE CHAFING DISH

菊
花
鍋
子

During the fall when the chrysanthemums are in season, this fragrant dish is very popular, either as a midnight snack or as refreshment when people gather for an evening of friendly conversation. One nice feature is that the guests prepare their own food, selecting from the variety of ingredients arranged around the dish. The Chinese chafing dish is similar to those used in the West except that charcoal is burned at the base to supply the necessary heat, and a chimney goes up through the center.

The ingredients given below are those used in China, but substitutions may easily be made to suit the fancy of the hostess.

1 chicken	*3 cups sliced celery cabbage*
7 cups water	*8 chicken livers, sliced*
3 tablespoons soy sauce	*2 cups sliced fish*
Salt to taste	*4 cups hot cooked rice*
1 bundle long rice	*6 eggs*
2 cups oil	*Petals of 4 large white*
3 cups spinach, cut in	* chrysanthemums*
* 1-inch lengths*	

Skin chicken and remove all the meat from the bones. Slice breast meat very thin. Cover chicken bones and dark meat with 7 cups of water and add soy sauce. Bring to a boil and simmer 20 minutes. Add salt to taste. Put half of the bundle of long rice to soak in cold water. Heat oil and deep fry the other half (page 19).

Arrange ingredients on separate plates around the chafing dish in the following order: vegetables, meats, rice, raw eggs, and chrysanthemum petals. Heat chafing dish and add half of the hot stock. Invite each guest to take his chopsticks and place portions of the ingredients in that section of the chafing dish directly in front of him, in the following order: (1) Add a portion of each vegetable and let simmer 2 minutes. (2) Add a portion of chicken and fish and let simmer 3 minutes. (3) Add some of the long rice. (4) Break an egg into the chafing dish to poach. (5) Add chrysanthemum petals. When the eggs are poached let each guest fill his bowl ¼ full of cooked rice and then add ingredients from the chafing dish.

If a second serving of the fragrant food is desired, pour the remaining stock into the chafing dish and repeat process. Serves 6.

GOLD COIN CHICKEN

金
錢
鷄

18 pieces of chicken, ¼ inch
  thick and cut the size and
  shape of a dollar
18 pieces of pork fat cut same
  as chicken
18 pieces of boiled ham cut
  same as chicken
6 pieces of wire 7 inches long

MIX: 2 tablespoons sugar (or
  honey)
½ teaspoon salt
1 tablespoon sherry
1 tablespoon soy sauce
1 teaspoon garlic juice
1 teaspoon fresh ginger
  juice

Marinate chicken 30 minutes or longer in mixture of sugar, salt, sherry, soy sauce, garlic juice, and ginger juice. Remove, and in the center of each piece of chicken, pork fat, and boiled ham cut a small square hole like the hole in an old Chinese coin. String alternate pieces of chicken, ham, and pork fat on piece of wire until there are three of each. Bend the wire so that the pieces are brought together. Repeat until the 6 pieces of wire have been used. Place in a baking pan and broil 20 minutes at 375° or until they are a rich, golden brown. Serve on platter. Serves 3.

The meat may be arranged on skewers for roasting over an open fire but this requires more patience.

LYCHEE CHICKEN

荔
枝
鷄

1 fryer (3 pounds)
10 water chestnuts
1 small onion, chopped fine
3 cups oil
1 can lychees

MIX: 2 tablespoons cornstarch
½ teaspoon salt
2 tablespoons soy sauce
2 teaspoons sherry
2 egg whites

Remove meat from bones and chop fine. Peel water chestnuts and chop fine. Combine chopped chicken, chestnuts, and onion and mix well. Add mixture of cornstarch, salt, soy sauce, sherry, and egg whites. Mix well and form into balls. Heat pan, add oil, and fry balls until brown. Drain. Arrange balls in a deep platter and garnish with lychees.

SAUCE

1 tablespoon oil
2 teaspoons cornstarch
1 tablespoon soy sauce

¼ cup chicken stock
½ cup lychee juice

Heat pan and add 1 tablespoon oil. Mix sauce ingredients and add. Boil 1 minute. Pour over chicken balls and serve.

Fresh lychees, with shell and seed removed, may be used instead of canned lychees.

PAPER-WRAPPED CHICKEN

紙
包
鷄

This is a famous Szechuen dish.

Breast meat of 1 fryer	*½ teaspoon garlic juice*
(3 pounds)	*1 teaspoon sherry*
1 teaspoon salt	*2 teaspoons sesame oil*
1 teaspoon sugar	*2 cups oil*
1 tablespoon soy sauce	*18 pieces of waxed paper, 6*
½ teaspoon ginger juice	*inches square*

Cut breast meat of chicken into strips 1 inch wide, then cut each strip diagonally into ½-inch pieces (76 pieces). Put chicken in bowl and add salt, sugar, soy sauce, ginger juice, garlic juice, sherry, and 2 teaspoons sesame oil. Mix well and let stand in refrigerator 30 minutes. Remove and wrap 4 pieces of chicken in each square of waxed paper. Heat 2 cups oil and deep fry packages 1½ minutes. Remove. Serve hot. The delicious flavor of the chicken will be ample reward for having to unwrap the packages at the table. Serves 6.

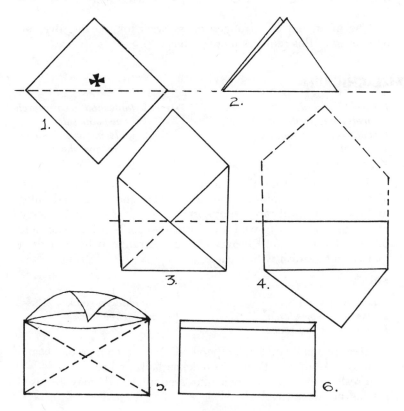

PINEAPPLE CHICKEN I

波
蘿
鷄

1 fryer (3 pounds)
½ cup pineapple tidbits
4 buttons garlic, crushed
½ cup pineapple juice
1 cup water
6 tablespoons oil
Parsley

MIX: 4 tablespoons soy sauce
1 teaspoon sherry
1 tablespoon sugar
½ teaspoon salt
1 tablespoon chopped
ginger

Wash chicken and rub inside and out with mixture of soy sauce, sherry, sugar, salt, and ginger. Let stand 20 minutes. Heat pan, add oil, and brown garlic. Add chicken and brown on both sides. Add remaining soy sauce mixture gradually. Add pineapple juice and water. Simmer 2 minutes. Remove chicken and sauce to deep pot, cover, and simmer 25 minutes.

Cut chicken into segments and arrange on platter (page 62). Garnish chicken with pineapple and parsley and pour hot sauce over the chicken. Serves 4.

If there is more than 1 cup of gravy it should be thickened with 1 tablespoon cornstarch mixed with 1 teaspoon water.

PINEAPPLE CHICKEN II

波
蘿
鷄

1 fryer (3 pounds)
½ cup pineapple tidbits
10 water chestnuts
4 tablespoons oil
1 cup sliced onions
2 cups sliced celery

4 tablespoons pineapple juice
MIX: 1 teaspoon cornstarch
1 teaspoon salt
2 teaspoons cold water
2 teaspoons soy sauce

Skin chicken and remove all the meat from the bones. Slice meat and liver diagonally. Marinate in mixture of cornstarch, salt, water, and soy sauce. Peel water chestnuts and slice. Heat pan, add 1 tablespoon oil, and sauté onions ½ minute. Remove. Reheat pan, add 1 tablespoon oil, and sauté celery and water chestnuts 1 minute. Remove. Reheat pan, add 2 tablespoons oil, and sauté chicken 2 minutes. Add vegetables, pineapple, and pineapple juice and cook 4 seconds. Be sure not to let vegetables burn or become too well cooked.

Mutton or beef may be substituted for chicken.

ROAST CHICKEN

燒
鷄

1 fryer (3¼ pounds)
1 cup soy sauce
1 tablespoon sherry
1 tablespoon honey
1 teaspoon salt

4 cloves garlic, crushed
1 tablespoon minced fresh
  ginger
¼ cup green onions, cut in
  ¼-inch lengths

Mix soy sauce, sherry, honey, salt, garlic, ginger, and green onions. Rub chicken inside and out with mixture and let stand 45 minutes. Remove chicken from soy sauce mixture and roast 55 minutes at 375° F., basting every 20 minutes with soy sauce mixture. Cut chicken into segments and arrange on platter (page 62). Serves 4.

SHERRY CHICKEN

鷄
酒

1 fryer (3 pounds)
4 tablespoons oil
1 cup sliced fresh ginger
2½ cups sherry
1½ cups water

MIX: 1 teaspoon soy sauce
4 tablespoons sugar
2 teaspoons salt
4 cloves garlic, crushed

Rub chicken with mixture of soy sauce, sugar, salt, and garlic. Heat pan, add oil, and fry chicken until light brown. Add ginger, sherry, water, and remaining soy sauce mixture. Bring to a boil and simmer 30 minutes. Remove chicken, cut into segments, and arrange on deep platter (page 62). Pour hot gravy over chicken. Serves 4.

SHERRY CHICKEN WITH MUSHROOMS

冬
菇
雞
酒

1 chicken (2½ pounds)
4 tablespoons oil
1 cup sherry
¾ cups sliced fresh ginger

1½ cups water
1½ teaspoons salt
1 4-ounce can whole mushrooms

Cut chicken into segments (page 62). Slice gizzard and liver. Heat pan, add oil, and sauté chicken 1 minute. Add sherry, ginger, water, salt, and mushrooms and simmer 20 minutes. Serves 2.

A half cup of sliced bamboo shoot may be added. Twelve dried mushrooms may be substituted for canned mushrooms. (See instructions for soaking and cleaning dried mushrooms, page 21).

SMOKED CHICKEN

焗
鷄

1 fryer (2½ pounds)
¼ cup soy sauce
1 teaspoon salt
¾ cup dark brown sugar

MIX: 1 tablespoon salt
2 cups water
1 piece aluminum foil, 15 x 30 inches

Rub chicken with soy sauce and salt and let stand 20 minutes. Bring water to a boil, add chicken, and simmer 20 minutes. Remove, let cool, and place in refrigerator overnight.

Put aluminum foil in a large sauce pan and put chicken in center. Place sugar beside chicken. Wrap the foil around the chicken, making sure it is well sealed. Cook over medium flame 45 minutes. (The color of the chicken will be rather dark due to the sugar.) Remove chicken, cut into segments, and arrange on platter (page 62).

SOY SAUCE CHICKEN

豉
油
雞

1 fryer (3½ pounds)
¾ cup soy sauce
1 tablespoon honey
½ cup brown sugar
1½ cups water
2 tablespoons chopped fresh ginger

3 cloves garlic, crushed
1 star anise
¼ cup green onions, cut in ½-inch lengths
2 tablespoons sherry
MIX: 2 tablespoons cornstarch
4 tablespoons water

Combine soy sauce, honey, sugar, water, ginger, garlic, anise, green onions, and sherry in a large pot. Bring to a boil and simmer 2 minutes. Add whole chicken, including gizzard and liver, and simmer 40 minutes. Remove chicken, cut into segments, and arrange on platter (page 62). Add mixture of cornstarch and water to gravy, bring to a boil, and simmer ½ minute. Pour over chicken. Serves 4.

SPRING CHICKEN AND PEPPERS

鷄
肉
炒
辣
椒

1 young chicken (1½ pounds)
1 red pepper, sliced
1 onion, sliced
1 cucumber, sliced (not peeled)
1 cup oil
1 tablespoon cornstarch
1 tablespoon soy sauce

MIX: 1 tablespoon cornstarch
½ teaspoon sugar
½ teaspoon salt
2 tablespoons soy sauce
¼ cup water or stock

Chop chicken into 2-inch segments (page 62). Combine corn-starch and soy sauce, add to chicken, and mix well. Add sliced pepper, onion, and cucumber to mixture of cornstarch, sugar, salt, soy sauce, and stock. Mix well. Heat pan and add oil. Fry chicken until brown, then remove to serving bowl. Pour off oil. Reheat pan and add 2 tablespoons oil. Sauté vegetables 2 minutes and pour over chicken. Serves 3.

SPRING CHICKEN AND TOMATOES

鷄
肉
炒
蕃
茄

1 young chicken (1½ pounds)
1 teaspoon cornstarch
1 tablespoon soy sauce
1 tablespoon sherry
½ cup oil
¾ cup cubed onions
1½ cups cubed tomatoes

MIX: 1 tablespoon cornstarch
1 teaspoon sugar
¼ teaspoon salt
½ cup water or chicken stock
1 tablespoon soy sauce

Skin chicken, remove meat from bones, and cut into cubes. Combine cornstarch, soy sauce, and sherry and pour over chicken. Heat pan, add oil and sauté chicken until brown. Add onions and fry 2 seconds. Remove and pour off oil. Reheat pan and add 2 tablespoons oil. Add mixture of cornstarch, sugar, salt, stock, and soy sauce. Bring to a boil, stirring constantly. Add chicken and onions and sauté 1 minute. Add tomatoes and stir well for 2 seconds. Serves 3.

STEWED CHICKEN

燉
鷄

2 chicken drumsticks
2 chicken thighs
2 chicken wings
2 tablespoons oil
1 button garlic, chopped
1 tablespoon chopped fresh ginger
⅓ cup sliced onion

2 tablespoons red bean curd
1½ tablespoons sugar
3 tablespoons soy sauce
½ teaspoon 5-Spice
2½ cups water
2 large potatoes, cut in 1-inch cubes

Cut drumsticks, thighs, and wings into 2-inch segments (page 62). Heat pan and add oil. Add garlic, ginger, and onion and brown well. Add bean curd and sauté 2 seconds. Add chicken and sauté 1 minute. Add sugar, soy sauce, 5-spice, and water. Simmer until chicken is tender (about 15 minutes). Add potatoes and continue cooking until potatoes are done. Serves 3.

STUFFED CHICKEN

釀
鷄

1 fryer (3½ pounds)
8 water chestnuts
4 dried mushrooms
1 whole bamboo shoot, cubed
¼ cup pearl barley
20 dried lotus seeds
2 tablespoons oil
¼ pound pork, cubed
¾ cup cubed raw ham
1 chicken gizzard, cubed

½ cup chicken stock
2 tablespoons soy sauce
1 tablespoon sherry
1 teaspoon salt
1 tablespoon lard
1 teaspoon sugar
3 tablespoons water in which
   mushrooms were soaked
2 slices ginger

Remove breast bones of chicken through opening in neck. Peel water chestnuts and cube. Soak dried mushrooms and clean (page 21). Squeeze dry and cube. Soak pearl barley 2 hours. Wash and boil 30 minutes. Wash dried lotus seeds and soak in 2 cups of water 1 hour. Bring to a boil in the same water and continue boiling 5 minutes. Pour off the water and let cool. Remove seed covering. Heat pan, add oil, and sauté chestnuts, mushrooms, bamboo shoot, barley, lotus seeds, pork, ham, and gizzard 2 minutes. Add chicken stock, soy sauce, sherry, salt, lard, sugar, mushroom liquid, and ginger. Simmer 4 minutes. Stuff chicken with this mixture and sew up opening. Place chicken in large bowl and steam 1 hour or until tender. Serves 4.

WALNUT CHICKEN

合
桃
鷄

1 fryer (3 pounds)
1 cup walnuts
2 cups oil
⅓ cup dried mushrooms
½ cup cubed bamboo shoots
½ cup cubed celery
¼ cup cubed onions

10 water chestnuts
⅓ cup chicken stock or water
MIX: 1 tablespoon cornstarch
   ¾ teaspoon salt
3 tablespoons soy sauce
2 tablespoons sherry

Skin chicken and remove the meat from the bones. Cut into ½-inch cubes and marinate in mixture of cornstarch, salt, soy sauce, and sherry. Blanch walnuts, remove skins, and deep fry. Remove and pour off oil. Soak mushrooms and clean (page 21). Squeeze dry and cube. Peel water chestnuts and cube. Heat pan, add 3 tablespoons oil, and sauté vegetables 1 minute. Remove. Reheat pan, add 4 tablespoons oil, and sauté chicken 2 minutes. Add vegetables and stock, mix well, and cook 2 minutes. Place on platter and garnish with fried walnuts. Serves 6.

A pound and a half of breast meat may be used instead of a whole chicken. A 4-ounce can of whole mushrooms may be substituted for dried mushrooms, and cashew nuts or blanched almonds may be used instead of walnuts.

DUCK

DUCK AND BAMBOO SHOOTS

竹
笋
鴨

1 duck (3½ pounds)
4 tablespoons oil
1 onion, sliced
2 buttons garlic, crushed
2 tablespoons crushed fresh
  ginger
2 canned bamboo shoots, sliced
3 cups water

MIX: 1 teaspoon cornstarch
½ teaspoon salt
1 tablespoon sugar
2 tablespoons sherry
3 tablespoons thick soy
  sauce (Tick Jee Yau)
4 tablespoons soy sauce

Cut duck in two and rub with mixture of cornstarch, salt, sugar, sherry, and soy sauce. Let stand 20 minutes. Heat pan and add oil. Fry onion, garlic, and ginger ½ minute. Add duck and fry on both sides until golden brown. Add water and any remaining sauce. Simmer 20 minutes. Add bamboo shoots and cook until duck is tender. Serves 6.

DUCK AND DRIED LILY BUDS

花
子
鴨

1 duck (3½ pounds)
½ cup dried lily buds
½ cup dried fungi
1 cup oil
½ cup sliced bamboo shoots
½ cup sliced mushrooms
2 cups water

MIX: 2 teaspoons sugar
1½ teaspoons salt
4 tablespoons soy sauce
3 tablespoons sherry
¼ cup ginger juice
¼ cup garlic juice

Rub duck with mixture of sugar, salt, soy sauce, sherry, ginger juice, and garlic juice. Let stand 20 minutes. Soak lily buds and fungi separately 10 minutes in 2 cups warm water each. Wash and pour off water. Heat pan, add oil, and brown duck. Remove duck and pour off oil. Reheat pan, add 2 tablespoons oil, and sauté lily buds, fungi, bamboo shoots, and mushrooms 1 minute. Add remaining soy sauce mixture and water and simmer 1 minute. Remove to large pot, add duck, and simmer until tender.

Bamboo shoots and mushrooms may be omitted if desired.

DUCK LIVER ROLLS

鴨
肝
卷

4 duck livers
1 large piece pork caul
1 tablespoon cornstarch
3 tablespoons water
⅓ cup dried mushrooms
8 water chestnuts
3¼ cups oil
1 small onion, sliced

¼ teaspoon salt
2 tablespoons soy sauce
1 tablespoon sherry
¾ teaspoon sugar
⅓ cup sliced bamboo shoots
½ teaspoon gourmet powder
2 cups flour

Scald duck livers and drain. Rub pork caul with paste made of cornstarch and water. Soak mushrooms and clean (page 21). Squeeze dry and slice. Peel water chestnuts and slice. Heat pan, add 4 tablespoons oil, and sauté livers 1 minute. Add onions, salt, soy sauce, sherry, and sugar. Sauté 3 seconds. Add sliced mushrooms, water chestnuts, and bamboo shoots and sauté 1 minute. Add gourmet powder and 1 tablespoon water and cook 1 second. Remove. Cut pork caul into 4 pieces 5 by 6 inches. Put ¼ of the cooked ingredients into each piece of caul, turn up the edges about 1 inch, and form into rolls. Spread flour on wax paper and cover each roll with as much flour as it will hold. Heat 3 cups oil and deep fry rolls, two at a time, until light brown. Remove to plate and cut in 2-inch pieces. Serves 3.

Egg Noodle dough (page 128) rolled paper thin and cut to the above dimensions may be substituted for pork caul. The dough, however, should not be covered with flour.

One cup of any of the following may be substituted for the duck livers: sliced chicken, chicken livers, pork, or shrimps.

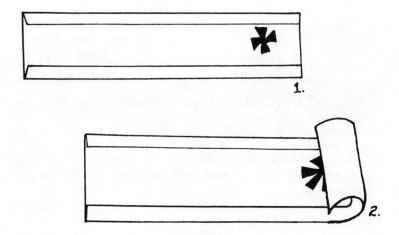

1.

2.

DUCK LIVERS ON TOAST

鴨
肝
多
士

6 duck livers, finely chopped
12 water chestnuts
1 egg white
1 tablespoon soy sauce
½ teaspoon salt

1 teaspoon sherry
5 slices bread, cut in
   2-inch squares
Parsley
2 cups oil

Peel water chestnuts, chop fine, and mix with chopped livers. Add unbeaten egg white, soy sauce, salt, and sherry. Spread on bread squares and decorate with parsley. Heat pan, add oil, and deep fry until brown. Serves 4.

Pork, chicken livers, or shrimps may be substituted for duck livers.

JADE BELT DUCK

玉
帶
鴨

1 duck (3½ pounds)
1 pound sliced ham
2 bunches leeks, chives, or
   young green onions
2 cups water

2 tablespoons sherry
3 tablespoons soy sauce
½ teaspoon salt
1 tablespoon crushed fresh
   ginger

Bring duck to a boil in 2 cups water and simmer 15 minutes. Remove to platter, saving stock. Cut duck in segments (page 62). Cut ham in 1 x 2-inch pieces. Tie a piece of ham to each piece of duck using the leeks as string. Arrange in a deep bowl. Add stock, sherry, soy sauce, salt, and ginger. Steam 1 hour or until duck is tender.

PINEAPPLE DUCK

波
蘿
鴨

1 duck (3½ pounds)
5 tablespoons oil
2 buttons garlic, crushed
3 cups water
½ cup pineapple juice
½ cup pineapple tidbits

MIX: 1 tablespoon sugar
¾ teaspoon salt
1 tablespoon chopped
   ginger
4 tablespoons soy sauce
1 teaspoon sherry

Rub duck with mixture of sugar, salt, ginger, soy sauce, and sherry. Heat pan, add oil, and sauté garlic until brown. Remove duck from sauce and brown on both sides. Add remaining sauce, water, and pineapple juice, and simmer until tender (about 1 hour). Remove duck from gravy, cut into segments, and arrange on platter (page 62). Garnish with pineapple tidbits and pour hot gravy over it.

Gravy may be thickened by adding 1½ tablespoons cornstarch mixed with 2 tablespoons water.

ROAST DUCK

燒
鴨

1 duck (3½ pounds)
½ cup soy sauce
3 tablespoons dark bean sauce
2 teaspoons ground cinnamon
½ cup green onions, cut in
    2-inch lengths
3 tablespoons dark brown sugar

4 cloves garlic, crushed
½ teaspoon 5-spice

MIX: ¼ cup soy sauce
2 teaspoons sugar
½ teaspoon garlic juice
½ teaspoon ginger juice

Wash duck and tie neck with string. Combine soy sauce, bean sauce, cinnamon, green onions, brown sugar, garlic, and 5-spice. Pour into the body cavity of the duck. Insert skewers across opening and lace tightly with cord to prevent sauce from running out. Place duck, breast up, on rack in shallow pan, and pour mixture of soy sauce, sugar, garlic and ginger juice over it. Roast uncovered in slow oven (360° F.) 1 hour, basting every 20 minutes with soy sauce mixture in the pan. Cut into segments and arrange on platter (page 62). Serves 4.

SWEET-SOUR DUCK LIVERS

甜
酸
鴨
肝

6 duck livers
1 cup oil
1 tablespoon soy sauce
¼ cup water
1 carrot sliced
1 onion, sliced

MIX: 3 teaspoons cornstarch
1 teaspoon soy sauce
2 teaspoons sherry

Cut each liver in two lengthwise and rub with mixture of cornstarch, soy sauce, and sherry. Heat pan, add oil, and deep fry livers until brown. Remove and pour off oil. Reheat pan, add soy sauce, water, and 3 tablespoons oil. Bring to a boil, add carrot and onion, and simmer 5 seconds.

SWEET-SOUR SAUCE

1 teaspoon cornstarch
4 tablespoons sugar
½ cup vinegar

1 teaspoon sherry
1 tablespoon soy sauce

Mix ingredients for sweet-sour sauce and add cooked carrot and onion. Bring to a boil and simmer 1 minute. Add livers. Serves 4.

Pieces of toast ½-inch square may be added with livers.

PIGEON

MINCED PIGEON

白
鴿
鬆

2 pigeons
8 water chestnuts
2 cups oil
½ bunch long rice
1 large onion, minced
1 stalk celery, minced
4 mushrooms, minced
½ cup minced bamboo shoot

3 tablespoons soy sauce
¼ cup chicken stock
1 tablespoon sugar
½ teaspoon salt
2 tablespoons sherry
MIX: 1 tablespoon cornstarch
2 tablespoons water

Clean and skin pigeons. Remove meat from bones and mince. Peel water chestnuts and mince. Heat pan, add oil, and fry long rice. Arrange on platter (page 19). Pour off the oil. Reheat pan, add 2 tablespoons oil, and sauté pigeon meat 30 seconds. Reheat pan, add 2 tablespoons oil, and sauté water chestnuts, onions, celery, mushrooms, and bamboo shoot 1 minute. Add soy sauce, chicken stock, sugar, salt, and sherry and simmer 1 minute. Add 2 tablespoons oil and mixture of cornstarch and water. Add pigeon and simmer 1 minute. Pour over long rice.

Shredded lettuce may be used instead of long rice.

FRIED SQUABS

炸
白
鴿

2 medium-sized squabs
¼ cup sliced onions
1 tablespoon crushed fresh
    ginger
3 cups oil

MIX: 3 tablespoons soy sauce
1 tablespoon sherry
½ teaspoon salt
2 teaspoons sugar
½ teaspoon 5-spice

Clean squabs and cut each into 4 pieces. Add mixture of soy sauce, sherry, salt, sugar, and 5-spice, and mix well. Add onions and ginger and let stand 2 hours. Heat pan, add oil, and deep fry squabs until brown. Serves 2.

MEATS

肉
類

Undoubtedly the Chinese of prehistoric times were great meat eaters. Recipes inscribed on bamboo and silk and wooden plaques indicate that 3500 years ago meat was a major item in their diet. By Confucius' time, however, it was beginning to be scarce. Today, meat is almost a luxury, used more often to flavor a dish than as a dish by itself. Since there are so few homes in China with ovens, roasted meat as Westerners know it is a delicacy bought from special shops or restaurants. Shops frequently sell as little as a single ounce of roasted pork.

A chain of circumstances has brought this about. The Chinese have a natural love for children, and this, plus their desire to have many descendants so they will be well loved while alive and well remembered after death, has caused a rapid and continuous increase in the population. As the population has increased, the size of individual farms has decreased. Today the agricultural economy of China is based on small family farms.

Domestic animals are more expensive to produce than vegetables and few family farms can support more than one or two. A cow eats so much that it competes with humans for grasses and grains. Arable land is too valuable to be used for pasturage, with the result that there are few herds of cattle. Furthermore, since refrigeration is extremely limited in China, and meat processing and packing are done only on a small scale, a cow raised for meat is a risky investment. A farmer who slaughters a cow must either sell most of the meat profitably or preserve it by drying, a rather large undertaking. Pigs forage for themselves and grow fat on any kind of food, so each small farm usually manages to support a few. Thus, pork has become the most common meat in China.

Mutton shares favor with pork in North China, and the Mongolian mutton grill is frequently seen. In South China much goat meat is eaten. The hilly terrain favors the raising of goats, which, like pigs, eat almost everything and forage for themselves.

The Chinese like the taste of meat, and recipes have been ingeniously devised to make small amounts of meat go as far as possible. Minced or thinly sliced in bite-size pieces — it is considered barbarous to carve meat at the table — it flavors the whole dish. Also, in such small pieces it is quickly cooked and thus saves fuel.

The quantities of meat called for in most of the following recipes will seem small, especially to American housewives accustomed to allowing at least one-half pound of meat per person.

BEEF

BEEF AND ASPARAGUS

露
笋
炒
牛
肉

½ pound beef, sliced
1¼ pound fresh asparagus
½ cup asparagus water
4 tablespoons oil
¼ cup shredded green onions

MIX: 1 teaspoon cornstarch
1 teaspoon sugar
½ teaspoon salt
2 teaspoons sherry
3 tablespoons soy sauce

Marinate the beef in the mixture of cornstarch, sugar, salt, sherry, and soy sauce. Snap off the tough part of the asparagus and cut each stalk into 2-inch pieces. Drop asparagus into 2 cups of boiling water and cook 5 minutes. Drain, saving ½ cup of water.

Heat pan, add 2 tablespoons oil, and sauté asparagus 4 minutes. Remove. Reheat pan, add 2 tablespoons oil, and sauté beef 4 seconds. Add asparagus and green onions and cook 1½ minutes. Add marinade and ½ cup asparagus water and cook 2 minutes longer. Serves 4.

BEEF AND BITTER MELON

苦
瓜
牛
肉

½ pound sliced beef
2 medium-sized bitter melons
2 tablespoons black beans
2 cloves garlic, crushed
½ cup water
6 tablespoons oil

MIX: 1 tablespoon cornstarch
¾ teaspoon salt
1 tablespoon sherry
2 tablespoons soy sauce
1 teaspoon fresh ginger
juice

Marinate beef in mixture of cornstarch, salt, sherry, soy sauce, and ginger juice. Cut each melon in two lengthwise. Remove seeds. Drop melon into 4 cups of boiling water and continue boiling 1 minute. With a teaspoon remove the white membrane inside the pieces of melon, then slice each piece diagonally into ⅛-inch pieces. (This should make about 2 cups.) Heat pan, add oil, and fry garlic 1 second. Add black beans and beef and sauté ½ minute. Add melon and water and sauté 2 minutes. Serves 4.

BEEF AND BROCCOLI

芥
蘭
牛
肉

½ pound beef, sliced
1 bunch of young broccoli
1 teaspoon crushed ginger
¼ cup water
1 clove garlic, crushed
4 tablespoons oil

MIX: 2 teaspoons cornstarch
¼ teaspoon salt
1 tablespoon sugar
1 tablespoon sherry
1 tablespoon soy sauce

Marinate meat in mixture of cornstarch, salt, sugar, sherry, and soy sauce. Peel stalks of broccoli. Drop broccoli into boiling water and parboil 1 minute. Remove and slice. (This should make about 2⅔ cups.) Heat pan, add 2 tablespoons oil, and sauté beef 2 seconds. Remove. Reheat pan, add 2 tablespoons oil, and sauté ginger, garlic, and broccoli 1 minute. Add beef and water and simmer 2 minutes. Serves 3.

BEEF AND CABBAGE

紹
菜
牛
肉

½ pound beef, sliced
4½ cups sliced cabbage
2 tablespoons oil

MIX: 1½ teaspoons salt
1 tablespoon sugar

1 tablespoon chopped
   ginger
3 tablespoons soy sauce
½ tablespoon sherry

Marinate beef in mixture of salt, sugar, ginger, soy sauce, and sherry. Drop cabbage into 5 cups of boiling water and parboil 2 minutes. Remove and drain. Heat pan and add oil. Remove beef from marinade and sauté 4 seconds. Add cabbage and sauté 1 minute. Add marinade, mix well, and cook 4 seconds. Serves 4.

BEEF AND CAULIFLOWER

牛
肉

½ pound beef, sliced
2 cups cauliflower flowerets
4 tablespoons oil
½ teaspoon salt
1 tablespoon soy sauce
⅓ cup water

MIX: 2 teaspoons cornstarch
1 teaspoon salt
2 tablespoons soy sauce
4 tablespoons water

椰
菜
花
炒

Marinate beef in mixture of cornstarch, salt, soy sauce, and water. Drop cauliflower into boiling water and parboil 1½ minutes. Remove. Heat pan, add 2 tablespoons oil, and sauté cauliflower 2 seconds. Add salt and soy sauce and sauté 1 minute. Remove. Reheat pan, add 2 tablespoons oil, and sauté beef 2 seconds. Add cauliflower, ⅛ cup water, and marinade and simmer 1 minute. Serves 3.

BEEF AND CORN

粟
米
炒
牛
肉

½ pound beef, diced
1¾ cups whole kernel corn,
    fresh or canned
6 tablespoons oil
¾ cup diced onions
¾ cup diced green peppers
¾ cup diced tomatoes
¼ cup water

MIX: 2 teaspoons cornstarch
1 teaspoon salt
4 tablespoons soy sauce
2 teaspoons sherry
2 cloves garlic, crushed
1 tablespoon crushed
    fresh ginger

Marinate beef in mixture of cornstarch, salt, soy sauce, sherry, garlic, and ginger. Heat pan and add 3 tablespoons oil. Remove beef from marinade and sauté 3 seconds. Remove. Reheat pan, add 3 tablespoons oil, and sauté corn, onions, and peppers 4 seconds. Add marinade, mix well, and sauté 3 seconds. Add meat, tomatoes, and water and cook 3 seconds. Serves 4.

Diced pork or raw shrimps may be substituted for beef.

BEEF AND LOTUS ROOT

蓮
藕
炒
牛
肉

1 cup sliced beef
2½ cups sliced lotus root
1 tablespoon cornstarch
¼ cup water
4 tablespoons oil

MIX: 3 tablespoons soy sauce
2 cloves garlic, crushed

1 tablespoon shredded
    green onions
½ tablespoon salt
1 tablespoon tomato
    catsup (optional)
⅛ tablespoon Tabasco
    Sauce (optional)

Marinate beef in mixture of soy sauce, garlic, green onions, salt, catsup, and Tabasco Sauce. Drop lotus root into 2 cups boiling water and parboil 2 minutes. Heat pan, add 4 tablespoons oil, and sauté beef 3 seconds. Stir in lotus root and mix well. Add any remaining marinade. Mix cornstarch and water and add to beef and lotus root. Cook 2 minutes. Serves 4.

BEEF AND MUSTARD CABBAGE

芥
菜
炒
牛
肉

½ pound sirloin tip, sliced
1 large mustard cabbage
3 tablespoons oil
¼ cup water

MIX: 2 teaspoons cornstarch
1 teaspoon sugar
1 teaspoon salt
1½ tablespoons soy sauce
1 teaspoon garlic or
ginger juice

Marinate the meat in mixture of cornstarch, sugar, salt, soy sauce, and garlic or ginger juice. Cut away the top leaves of the cabbage (about 6 inches) leaving mostly the stalks. Slice stalks diagonally. (This should make about 4 cups.) Drop cabbage into 3 cups boiling water and parboil 1 minute. Remove. Heat pan and add oil. Add meat and marinade and sauté ½ minute. Add cabbage and stir 2 seconds. Add water and simmer ½ minute. Serves 3.

BEEF AND ONIONS

洋
葱
炒
牛
肉

½ pound beef, sliced
2 large onions, sliced
4 tablespoons oil
¼ cup water

MIX: 2 teaspoons cornstarch
½ teaspoon salt
½ teaspoon sugar
2 tablespoons soy sauce
2 teaspoons sherry

Marinate beef in mixture of cornstarch, salt, sugar, soy sauce, and sherry. Heat pan, add 2 tablespoons oil, and sauté beef 2 seconds. Remove. Reheat pan, add 2 tablespoons oil, and sauté onions 1 minute. Add beef and water and cook 3 seconds. Serves 4.

Oyster sauce may be used instead of soy sauce.

BEEF AND OYSTER SAUCE

蠔
油
牛
肉

1 pound beef, sliced
3 tablespoons oyster sauce
4 tablespoons oil
2 teaspoons sugar
¼ teaspoon pepper

1 tablespoon cornstarch
1 teaspoon sherry
1 teaspoon gourmet powder
6 tablespoons water
1 onion, sliced thin

Heat pan, add oil, and sauté beef 6 seconds. Mix oyster sauce, sugar, pepper, cornstarch, sherry, gourmet powder, and water and add to beef. Add onion and stir ½ minute. Serves 3.

BEEF AND PICKLED MUSTARD CABBAGE

咸
酸
菜
炒
牛
肉

½ pound beef, sliced
2 cups pickled mustard
    cabbage
3 tablespoons oil
2 tablespoons water

MIX: 2 teaspoons cornstarch
    2 tablespoons sugar
    4 tablespoons soy sauce
    4 tablespoons vinegar

Marinate beef in mixture of cornstarch, sugar, soy sauce, and vinegar. Heat pan, add oil and sauté beef 2 seconds. Add mustard cabbage and water and cook 2 minutes. Serves 4.

BEEF AND RADISHES

紅
蘿
蔔
炒
牛
肉

½ pound beef, sliced
1 teaspoon cornstarch
2 tablespoons soy sauce
1½ cups radishes (not peeled),
    sliced crosswise
4 tablespoons oil
¼ cup chopped green onions

MIX: 1 tablespoon cornstarch
    ½ cup sugar
    ⅓ cup vinegar
    4 tablespoons water

Combine cornstarch and soy sauce, add to beef and mix well. Heat pan and add oil. Add mixture of cornstarch, sugar, vinegar, and water and bring to a boil. Add radishes and simmer until they become transparent. Stir in beef and marinade and simmer 3 seconds. Add green onions and stir 1 second. Serves 4.

BEEF AND STRING BEANS

豆
角
炒
牛
肉

½ pound beef, sliced
½ pound string beans, sliced
    diagonally
3 tablespoons oil
¼ cup string bean water

MIX: 1 tablespoon cornstarch
    1 teaspoon sugar
    ½ teaspoon salt
    2 tablespoons soy sauce
    1 tablespoon sherry

Marinate beef in mixture of cornstarch, sugar, salt, soy sauce, and sherry. Heat pan, add 2 tablespoons oil, and sauté beef 2 seconds. Remove. Drop string beans into 1½ cups boiling water and parboil 1 minute. Drain, saving ¼ cup of the water. Heat pan, add 1 tablespoon oil, and sauté string beans 1 minute. Add beef and ¼ cup water from string beans and cook ½ minute, stirring well. Serves 4.

BEEF AND TOMATOES

蕃
茄
牛
肉

1 cup sliced beef
2 cups sliced tomatoes
5 tablespoons oil
4 cloves garlic, crushed
2 cups sliced onions
1 teaspoon gourmet powder
½ cup water

MIX: 1 tablespoon cornstarch
¾ teaspoon salt
3 teaspoons sugar
⅛ teaspoon pepper
3 tablespoons soy sauce

Marinate beef in mixture of cornstarch, salt, sugar, pepper and soy sauce. Heat pan, add 3 tablespoons oil, and fry garlic until brown. Add beef and sauté 1 minute. Remove. Reheat pan, add 2 tablespoons oil, and fry onions 1 minute. Add beef and sauté ½ minute. Add water and mix well. Stir in tomatoes and cook 1 minute.

Oyster sauce may be substituted for soy sauce.

BEEF AND VEGETABLES (CHOP SUEY)

菜
炒
牛
肉

¾ pound beef, sliced
1 cup sliced string beans
1 cup sliced carrots
1 cup sliced cauliflower
1 cup Chinese peas
1 cup sliced celery
½ cup water from vegetables
6 tablespoons oil

MIX: 1 tablespoon cornstarch
1 teaspoon salt
Few grains pepper
2 teaspoons sherry
3 tablespoons soy sauce
2 teaspoons
Worcestershire Sauce
2 buttons garlic, crushed
(optional)
1 tablespoon ginger juice
(optional)

Marinate beef in mixture of cornstarch, salt, pepper, sherry, soy sauce, Worcestershire Sauce, garlic, and ginger juice. Drop string beans and carrots into 1 cup of boiling water and parboil 1 minute. Remove. Drop cauliflower in the same water and parboil 1½ minutes. Remove. Drop Chinese peas in the same water and remove almost immediately (1 second). Drain, saving ½ cup of the water. Heat pan, add 3 tablespoons oil, and sauté vegetables 1 minute. Remove. Reheat pan and add 3 tablespoons oil. Remove beef from marinade and sauté 4 seconds. Add vegetables and mix well. Add marinade and ½ cup vegetable water and cook 1 minute. Serves 4.

Sliced chicken or prawns or shrimps sliced lengthwise may be substituted for beef. Other vegetables may be substituted for those listed.

BEEF AND WHITE CABBAGE

白菜炒牛肉

½ cup sliced beef
5 cups sliced white cabbage
4 tablespoons oil
½ cup water
1 teaspoon gourmet powder
¼ cup green onions, cut in
    ¼-inch lengths

MIX: ½ teaspoon cornstarch
1 teaspoon sugar
1 teaspoon salt
2 tablespoons soy sauce
2 teaspoons sherry

Marinate beef in mixture of cornstarch, sugar, salt, soy sauce, and sherry. Heat pan and add 2 tablespoons oil. Add cabbage, water, and gourmet powder. Bring to a boil and simmer 1 minute. Remove. Reheat pan, add 2 tablespoons oil, and fry onions 1 second. Add beef and sauté 4 seconds. Add cabbage and cook 2 minutes. Serves 3.

MEAT BALLS

肉丸

1 pound ground beef or pork
¾ cup mochi rice
MIX: 1 tablespoon soy sauce
    4 tablespoons hot water

MIX: ½ teaspoon salt
2 tablespoons cornstarch
3 tablespoons soy sauce
2 tablespoons sherry
3 tablespoons oil

Wash mochi rice and soak in 2 cups of water 1 hour. Drain. Add mixture of salt, cornstarch, soy sauce, sherry, and oil to beef and mix well. Form into balls about 1½ inches in diameter. Roll meat balls in mochi rice, coating well. Place in bowl and steam 35 minutes. Pour mixture of soy sauce and water over meat balls and steam 10 minutes longer.

POT ROAST

紅燒牛肉

1½ pounds beef pot roast
3 tablespoons oil
6 cloves garlic, crushed
2 tablespoons vinegar
2½ cups water

MIX: 1 teaspoon salt
½ teaspoon 5-spice
2 tablespoons brown
    sugar
4 tablespoons soy sauce

Heat pan and add oil. Add garlic and brown slightly. Add beef and brown on all sides. Add mixture of salt, 5-spice, brown sugar, and soy sauce. Cook 1 minute. Add vinegar and water and bring to a boil. Cover and simmer 1 hour. Remove meat and slice. Arrange on platter and pour hot gravy over it. Serves 3.

SOY SAUCE SHIN MEAT

豉
油
牛
肉

1 pound shin meat
2 cloves garlic, crushed
1 teaspoon crushed fresh ginger
1 anise
6 tablespoons dark brown sugar

½ teaspoon 5-spice
½ cup sliced onion
2 cups water
¾ cup soy sauce

Put all ingredients except the meat in a saucepan, bring to a boil, and simmer 2 minutes. Add meat and simmer 1 hour. Remove meat and slice. Arrange on platter and pour the hot sauce over it. Serves 3.

STEAMED MINCED BEEF

蒸
牛
肉
餅

¾ pound ground beef
½ cup dried salted Chinese
    white turnips
1 teaspoon chopped ginger

MIX: 3 tablespoons soy sauce
1½ teaspoons sherry
1 tablespoon sugar
2 tablespoons oil

Add mixture of soy sauce, sherry, sugar, and oil to ground beef and mix well. Add ginger and mix well. Wash salted turnips and chop very fine. Add to ground beef mixture. Place in bowl and steam 20 minutes. Serves 4.

PORK

BARBECUED SPARERIBS

紅
燒
排
骨

2½ pounds spareribs
¼ cup Black Sauce (Tick
    Jee Yau)
½ cup brown sugar
4 cloves garlic, crushed

1 tablespoon ginger juice
¼ cup sherry
1 square red bean curd
1½ cups water

Add water to spareribs, bring to a boil, and continue boiling until water evaporates. Remove to a bowl, and add Black Sauce, brown sugar, garlic, ginger juice, sherry, and bean curd. Mix well and let stand ½ hour. Bake in 8 x 12-inch pan 1 hour, at 350° F., basting with Black Sauce after 30 minutes.

BRAISED HAM

紅燒肘子

2 pounds picnic shoulder ham
4 tablespoons oil
4 tablespoons brown sugar
1 tablespoon sliced fresh ginger
2 green onions, cut in 3-inch
    lengths
½ cup water

MIX: 6 tablespoons soy sauce
2 tablespoons sherry
1 teaspoon salt

Add 3 cups of water to the ham, bring to a boil, and continue boiling 10 minutes. Remove, drain, and rub with mixture of soy sauce, sherry, and salt. Heat pan, add oil, and stir in sugar to make syrup. Add ginger and onions. Add ham and brown well. Add water and remaining soy sauce mixture. Simmer 1 minute. Remove ham and sauce to a large deep bowl and steam 1 hour or until tender. Serves 4.

MEAT DUMPLINGS

炸盒子

These dumplings may be made with either salty or sweet filling.

2 cups flour
¾ cup boiling water
2 cups oil

Add boiling water to flour gradually. Mix well until all the flour is absorbed. Roll out very thin on floured board. Cut with 2-inch cookie cutter. Put 1 teaspoonful of filling in the center of one circle, cover with another, and pinch edges together. Repeat until all the dough is used. Heat oil and deep fry dumplings, a few at a time, until light brown.

SALTY FILLING

1 cup ground pork
½ cup chopped bamboo shoots
1 tablespoon chopped onion
2 tablespoons oil

1 teaspoon salt
3 tablespoons soy sauce
1 tablespoon sherry

Combine pork and vegetables. Add oil, salt, soy sauce, and sherry, and mix well.

SWEET FILLING

1 cup chopped red roast pork
3 tablespoons green onions, cut
    in ½-inch lengths

1 tablespoon soy sauce
¼ teaspoon sugar

Combine ingredients and mix well.

LION'S HEAD

獅
子
頭

1½ pounds ground pork
6 dried mushrooms
8 water chestnuts
1 egg
1 tablespoon sherry
3 tablespoons soy sauce

½ teaspoon salt
2 tablespoons cornstarch
2 tablespoons sugar
4 cups oil
6 cups sliced celery cabbage
1½ cups chicken stock

Soak mushrooms and clean (page 21). Squeeze dry and chop. Peel water chestnuts and chop. Mix pork, mushrooms, and water chestnuts. Beat egg until lemon-colored and add to pork mixture. Add sherry, soy sauce, salt, cornstarch, and sugar. Mix well and form into 3 large flattened balls about 2 inches thick (similar to large hamburgers). Heat pan, add oil, and deep fry each ball until brown. Remove. Put sliced cabbage in a large pot, add stock, and put meat balls on top of cabbage. Cover and simmer ½ hour. Serves 4.

PEKING MEAT DUMPLINGS

北
平
餃
子

3 cups flour
1 cup water

½ cup soy sauce
3 tablespoons vinegar

Add half of the water to the flour and mix well. Add remaining water and knead well, until dough does not stick to the hands. Roll very thin on floured board and cut with 2-inch cookie cutter. Put 1 tablespoon of filling in the center of each circle, fold over and pinch edges together.

Bring to a boil the water in which the celery cabbage was cooked (see Filling below). Drop 18 dumplings into the boiling water and simmer 6 minutes. Remove dumplings to platter, placing them far enough apart so that they will not stick to each other. Repeat until all are cooked.

Combine soy sauce and vinegar and pour over dumplings.

FILLING

1 pound ground pork
1 large head celery cabbage
 (3½ pounds)
1 onion, minced

½ cup chives, cut in ⅛-inch
 lengths
4 tablespoons sesame oil
3 tablespoons soy sauce
1 tablespoon salt

Cut celery cabbage crosswise into 1-inch lengths. Bring 12 cups water to a boil, add celery cabbage, cover, and simmer 10 minutes. Remove cabbage and let cool, saving the water. Place cabbage in cheesecloth and squeeze out all the water. Chop cabbage very fine, return to cheesecloth, and again squeeze out water. Remove to large bowl. Heat pan, add 1 tablespoon sesame oil, and sauté onion and pork 1 minute. Add 3 tablespoons sesame oil, chives, soy sauce, and salt. Stir 2 minutes. Add to chopped cabbage and mix well.

The water in which the celery cabbage and dumplings were boiled may be seasoned to taste with salt and 1 teaspoon gourmet powder and served as soup.

These dumplings, instead of being boiled, may be pan fried until brown on both sides, or steamed 45 minutes, or deep fried and served as appetizers.

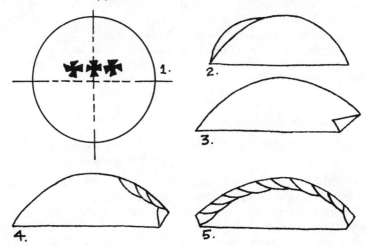

PINEAPPLE SPARERIBS

波
蘿
排
骨

1 pound spareribs
½ cup pineapple tidbits
3 tablespoons oil
3 cloves garlic, crushed
2 tablespoons preserved Chinese
    black beans
1 tablespoon preserved soy bean
    cake

2 tablespoons soy sauce
¼ cup dark brown sugar
½ cup pineapple juice
½ cup vinegar
¼ cup water
MIX: 2 teaspoons cornstarch
    1 tablespoon water

Have butcher cut spareribs into 2-inch pieces. Heat pan, add oil, and sauté garlic, black beans, and bean cake 3 seconds. Add spareribs and sauté 1 minute. Stir in soy sauce and brown sugar and cook 4 minutes. Add pineapple juice, vinegar, and water. Bring to a boil and simmer 20 minutes. Add pineapple and mixture of cornstarch and water and simmer 2 minutes. Serves 3.

PINEAPPLE SPARERIBS WITH SWEET-SOUR SAUCE

甜
酸
排
骨

1 pound spareribs
½ cup water
2 cups oil
4 lettuce leaves
½ cup pineapple tidbits

MIX: 1 tablespoon cornstarch
2 teaspoons soy sauce

Have butcher cut spareribs into 2-inch pieces. Add ½ cup water to spareribs, bring to a boil, and continue boiling uncovered until the water has evaporated. Remove to plate and rub with mixture of soy sauce and cornstarch. Heat oil and deep fry spareribs until medium brown and crisp. Remove and drain. Arrange on platter garnished with lettuce leaves. Garnish with pineapple tidbits.

SWEET-SOUR SAUCE

1 tablespoon cornstarch
½ cup dark brown sugar
⅓ cup vinegar

6 tablespoons pineapple juice
2 teaspoons soy sauce

Put cornstarch and brown sugar in saucepan. Add vinegar, pineapple juice, and soy sauce. Bring to a boil and simmer 1½ minutes. Pour over spareribs. Serves 3.

PORK AND BAMBOO SHOOTS

竹
笋
炒
猪
肉

½ pound lean pork, sliced
10 tablespoons oil
2 cups sliced bamboo shoots
¼ cup green onions, cut in
    1-inch lengths
½ cup water or stock

MIX: 1 tablespoon cornstarch
½ teaspoon salt
2 tablespoons soy sauce
2 tablespoons sherry

Marinate pork in mixture of cornstarch, salt, soy sauce, and sherry. Heat pan, add 8 tablespoons oil, and sauté bamboo shoots 1 minute. Remove. Reheat pan, add 2 tablespoons oil, and sauté pork ½ minute. Add bamboo shoots, green onions, and water. Simmer 1 minute. Serves 4.

PORK AND CELERY

猪
肉

½ pound shoulder pork, sliced
1 pound celery stalks, sliced
    diagonally
6 tablespoons oil

MIX: 1 tablespoon cornstarch
1 teaspoon sherry
1 tablespoon soy sauce
MIX: ½ teaspoon salt
1 teaspoon sherry
2 tablespoons soy sauce
¼ cup stock

炒
芹
菜

Marinate sliced pork in mixture of cornstarch, sherry, and soy sauce. Heat pan, add 4 tablespoons oil, and sauté pork 1 minute. Remove. Reheat pan, add 2 tablespoons oil, and sauté celery ½ minute. Add mixture of salt, sherry, soy sauce, and stock. Add pork and cook ½ minute. Serves 4.

PORK AND CHESTNUTS

栗
子
炒
猪
肉

1½ pounds lean pork
18 chestnuts
2 tablespoons oil
¾ cup sliced onion
1 tablespoon crushed fresh
   ginger
2 cups water

MIX: 4 tablespoons brown
   sugar
¼ teaspoon salt
6 tablespoons soy sauce
1 tablespoon sherry

Cut pork into ½-inch cubes. Shell chestnuts, remove skins, and cut each chestnut into halves. Heat pan and add oil. Add pork, onion, and ginger and sauté ½ minute. Add mixture of sugar, salt, soy sauce, and sherry and cook 1 minute. Add chestnuts and water and simmer until chestnuts are tender. Serves 6.

PORK AND CUCUMBERS

黃
瓜
炒
猪
肉

¼ pound shoulder pork, sliced
2 cucumbers (1 pound)
2 tablespoons oil
4 tablespoons water

MIX: ¼ teaspoon cornstarch
½ teaspoon salt
2½ teaspoons soy sauce

Marinate pork in mixture of cornstarch, salt, and soy sauce. Peel cucumbers, cut in two lengthwise, and slice diagonally about ¼ inch thick. (There should be about 3½ cups.) Heat pan, add oil, and sauté pork ½ minute. Add cucumbers and water and simmer 1½ minutes. Serves 4.

PORK AND GINGER ROOTS

子
羗
炒
猪
肉

½ pound pork, sliced
2 tablespoons oil
¾ cup sliced onion
¼ pound fresh young ginger
   roots, sliced
2 tablespoons water

MIX: 1 teaspoon cornstarch
1 teaspoon sugar
3 tablespoons soy sauce

Marinate pork in mixture of cornstarch, sugar, and soy sauce. Heat pan, add oil, and sauté pork and onion 1 minute. Add ginger and sauté ½ minute. Add water, mix well, and cook ½ minute. Serves 2.

PORK AND GOLDEN LILY BUDS

黄
花
子
炒
猪
肉

1 cup sliced pork
¾ cup dried golden lily buds
1½ cups dried fungi
3 tablespoons oil
¼ cup water

MIX: 1 teaspoon salt
2 teaspoons sugar
1 tablespoon sherry
2 tablespoons soy sauce

Soak fungi and lily buds separately in 1 cup water each for 20 minutes. Wash thoroughly. Heat pan, add oil, and sauté pork 1 minute. Add mixture of salt, sugar, sherry, and soy sauce. Add lily buds, fungi, and water. Mix well and cook 1½ minutes. Serves 6.

PORK AND PEAS

青
豆
炒
猪
肉

½ pound loin pork, sliced
1 cup Chinese peas
7 dried mushrooms
2 tablespoons oil
2 tablespoons soy sauce
1 teaspoon salt
1 tablespoon sherry

MIX: 1 tablespoon cornstarch
½ cup stock

Drop Chinese peas in boiling water and remove almost at once. Soak mushrooms and remove stems (page 21). Squeeze dry and slice. Heat pan, add oil, and sauté pork 1 minute. Add soy sauce, salt, and sherry and sauté ½ minute. Add peas and mushrooms. Add mixture of cornstarch and stock and cook 1 minute. Serves 2.

A 4-ounce can of button mushrooms may be substituted for dried mushrooms.

PORK AND PRESERVED CUCUMBERS

茶
瓜
炒
猪
肉

1 cup ground pork
12 large water chestnuts
⅓ cup chopped preserved cucumbers
1 cup chopped bamboo shoot

MIX: ½ teaspoon salt
1½ teaspoons sugar
2 tablespoons soy sauce
2 tablespoons oil
1 tablespoon sherry

Marinate pork in mixture of salt, sugar, soy sauce, oil, and sherry. Peel water chestnuts and chop. Add water chestnuts, cucumbers, and bamboo shoot to pork. Place in deep bowl and steam 30 minutes. Serves 4.

PORK AND RED BEAN CURD

紅
南
乳
肉

1½ pounds belly pork
4 tablespoons oil
1 small piece fresh ginger, sliced
2 buttons garlic, crushed
1 small onion, sliced

1 large piece red bean curd
4 tablespoons.soy sauce
3 tablespoons sugar
¼ teaspoon salt
3 cups water

Bring pork to a boil in 2 cups of water and continue boiling 10 minutes. Remove and let cool. Heat pan, add oil, and sauté ginger, garlic, and onion until brown. Add pork and sauté 3 minutes. Add bean curd, soy sauce, sugar, and salt and sauté 1 minute. Add water and simmer 45 minutes or until pork is tender. Serves 3.

PORK AND SHRIMP SAUCE (SAUTEED)

咸
蝦
醬
炒
豬
肉

This is a favorite Cantonese dish.

1 pound belly pork
2 tablespoons oil
4 cloves garlic, chopped
1 onion sliced
¼ cup green onions, cut in
    ½-inch lengths

2 tablespoons soy sauce
1 tablespoon sugar
2 tablespoons shrimp sauce
2½ cups water

Add 1½ cups of water to the pork, bring to a boil, and simmer 10 minutes. Remove and cut into 2-inch pieces. Heat pan, add oil, and sauté garlic and onions until light brown. Add pork and sauté ½ minute. Add soy sauce, sugar, and shrimp sauce and sauté 1 minute. Add 2½ cups water and simmer until tender (about 45 minutes). Serves 4.

PORK AND SHRIMP SAUCE (STEAMED)

咸
蝦
醬
蒸
豬
肉

½ pound pork, sliced
2 cloves garlic, crushed
2 tablespoons green onions, cut
    in ½-inch lengths

¾ teaspoon sugar
1 tablespoon shrimp sauce
1 tablespoon soy sauce
1 teaspoon crushed fresh ginger

Place sliced pork in deep bowl. Add the other ingredients and steam 25 minutes (page 23). Serves 2.

PORK AND TARO

芋
頭
猪
肉

1 pound pork, sliced
2 cups cubed taro
4 tablespoons oil
3 cloves garlic, crushed
4 pieces preserved bean cake
2 tablespoons green onions,
    cut in ¼-inch lengths

2 teaspoons red coloring
2 tablespoons soy sauce
1 tablespoon sugar
2 teaspoons sherry

MIX: 1 tablespoon cornstarch
     1 cup water

Heat pan, add oil, and fry garlic until light brown. Add bean cake and sauté 2 seconds. Add pork and sauté 1 minute. Add green onions, red coloring, soy sauce, sugar, and sherry. Stir 2 minutes. Add taro and mixture of cornstarch and water and simmer 30 minutes. Serves 4.

PORK, FUNGI, AND EGGS

炒
木
須
肉

½ cup sliced pork
12 fungi
4 eggs
4 tablespoons oil
3 tablespoons water
¼ cup green onions, cut in
    1-inch lengths

MIX: 1 teaspoon cornstarch
     ½ teaspoon salt
     1 tablespoon sherry
     3 tablespoons soy sauce

Marinate pork in mixture of cornstarch, salt, sherry, and soy sauce. Soak fungi in 1 cup hot water 5 minutes. Wash thoroughly. Break eggs into bowl and beat slightly. Heat pan and add 2 tablespoons oil. Add eggs and scramble. Remove. Reheat pan and add 2 tablespoons oil. Add pork and fungi and sauté 2 minutes. Add water, scrambled eggs, and green onions and cook 1 minute. Serves 4.

This is also known as "Scallion Pork."

PORK HASH

肉
餅

½ pound ground pork
3 water chestnuts
2 tablespoons green onions, cut
    in ¼-inch lengths
2 teaspoons soy sauce

1 teaspoon sugar
1 teaspoon sherry
1 teaspoon cornstarch
¼ teaspoon salt

Peel water chestnuts and crush. Combine all ingredients and mix well. Put in a deep bowl and steam 25 minutes. Serves 2.

PORK HASH AND EGGS

鷄
蛋
肉
餅

½ pound ground pork
4 eggs
½ teaspoon salt
2 teaspoons soy sauce
8 water chestnuts

2 tablespoons oil
¼ cup green onions, cut in
    ¼-inch lengths
½ cup cold water

Combine salt and soy sauce, add to pork, and mix well. Beat eggs with fork until lemon-colored. Peel water chestnuts and crush. Heat pan, add oil, and sauté pork 2 minutes. Remove to bowl and let cool. Add eggs, water chestnuts, onions, and water. Mix well and steam 30 minutes. Serves 4.

If water chestnuts are not available ¼ cup of chopped onions, celery, or Chinese yams may be substituted.

PORK HASH AND DRIED SQUID

鮂
魚
肉
餅

½ pound ground pork
¼ pound dried squid
4 water chestnuts
1½ tablespoons soy sauce

½ teaspoon salt
1 teaspoon sugar
1 tablespoon sherry
1 teaspoon ginger juice

Soak squid (page 21). Peel water chestnuts and crush. Combine all ingredients and mix well. Put in a deep bowl and steam 30 minutes. Serves 3.

PORK HASH AND PRESERVED CHINESE CUCUMBERS

冲
菜
蒸
猪
肉
餅

¾ pound ground pork
8 water chestnuts
2 tablespoons green onions,
    cut in ½-inch lengths
⅓ cup chopped preserved
    cucumbers
¼ cup chopped canned
    mushrooms

3 tablespoons soy sauce
3 teaspoons sherry
1 tablespoon oil
1 teaspoon sugar
1 teaspoon cornstarch

Peel water chestnuts and crush. Mix pork, water chestnuts, green onions, cucumbers, and mushrooms. Add soy sauce, sherry, oil, sugar, and cornstarch. Steam in deep bowl 25 minutes. Serves 4.

Chung Choy (salted turnip tops) may be substituted for cucumbers. Soak in 1 cup of water for 10 minutes, wash, and chop fine.

PORK HASH AND PRESERVED BLACK BEANS

豆
豉
肉
餅

½ pound ground pork
1 tablespoon crushed preserved
    black beans
1 tablespoon green onions, cut
    in ¼-inch lengths

1 tablespoon soy sauce
1 teaspoon sherry
1½ teaspoons sugar
½ teaspoon salt

Combine all ingredients and mix well. Put in a deep bowl and steam 25 minutes. Serves 2.

PORK HASH AND SALTED FISH

咸
魚
肉
餅

½ pound ground pork
1 tablespoon chopped salted
    fish
1 teaspoon sugar

½ teaspoon cornstarch
1 tablespoon green onions, cut
    in ¼-inch lengths

Combine all ingredients and mix well. Put in a deep bowl and steam 40 minutes. Serves 2.

PORK HASH AND SZECHUEN CHOY

炸
菜
肉
餅

Szechuen *choy* is also known as preserved Chungking cabbage. The vegetable is preserved by drying in the sun with salt and pepper added. The pepper gives it a special flavor.

½ pound ground pork
½ cup chopped Szechuen choy
¼ cup green onions, cut in
    ¼-inch lengths

3 tablespoons soy sauce
2 teaspoons sugar
1½ teaspoons sherry
¼ teaspoon salt

Wash Szechuen *choy* slightly before chopping. Combine all ingredients and mix well. Put in a deep bowl and steam 30 minutes. Serves 2.

PORK HASH AND WATER CHESTNUTS

馬
蹄
肉
餅

1 pound ground pork
10 water chestnuts
3 dried mushrooms
1 onion, chopped

3 tablespoons soy sauce
½ teaspoon salt
1 teaspoon cornstarch
2 tablespoons oil

Peel water chestnuts and chop. Soak dried mushrooms and clean (page 21)). Squeeze dry and chop. Mix pork, water chestnuts, mushrooms and onion. Add soy sauce, salt, cornstarch, and oil. Put in deep bowl and steam 25 minutes. Serves 4.

PORK, TAOFU, AND PEAS

豆
付
青
豆
炒
猪
肉

1½ cups diced pork
1 block taofu
2 cups frozen peas
2 tablespoons soy sauce
1 tablespoon sugar
½ teaspoon salt
1 teaspoon fresh ginger juice
   (optional)

4 small red chili peppers, diced
2 tablespoons Hoy Sien Jeung
2 cups oil
2 cloves garlic, crushed
1 onion, diced
MIX: 1 tablespoon cornstarch
   ⅓ cup water

Add soy sauce, sugar, salt, ginger juice, chili peppers, and Hoy Sien Jeung to pork and mix well. Cut taofu into 6 slices and each slice into 12 pieces. Heat pan, add oil, and deep fry taofu until medium brown. Remove and pour off oil. Reheat pan, add 4 tablespoons oil, and fry garlic and onion until brown. Add pork and sauté 2 minutes. Add peas and bean curd, and stir well 2 seconds. Add mixture of cornstarch and water, and sauté 1 minute. Serves 4.

RED ROAST PORK

叉
燒

1 pound lean pork
3 tablespoons crushed fresh
   ginger
½ cup green onions, cut in
   1-inch lengths
½ cup sliced round onions
6 cloves garlic, crushed
1 tablespoon honey

MIX: ½ teaspoon salt
   ¼ cup sugar
   ⅓ cup soy sauce
   2 tablespoons sherry
   1 teaspoon 5-spice
   (optional)
   2 teaspoons red coloring

Rub pork with mixture of salt, sugar, soy sauce, sherry, 5-spice, and coloring. Add ginger, green and round onions, garlic, and honey. Let stand ½ hour. Roast in oven at 425° F. for 15 minutes. Baste and continue cooking at 375° for 30 minutes. Remove. Cut roast pork into 2-inch wide strips and slice diagonally. Arrange on platter and pour remaining sauce over it. Serves 4.

RED ROAST PORK AND TAOFU

豆
付

2 cups sliced red roast pork
2 cups taofu, cut in 1-inch
   squares
4 tablespoons oil
1½ cups water
½ cup green onions, cut in
   ½-inch lengths

MIX: 1 tablespoon cornstarch
   ½ teaspoon salt
   2 tablespoons soy sauce
   2 tablespoons sherry

紅
叉
燒

Heat pan, add oil, and sauté taofu 1 minute. Add mixture of cornstarch, salt, soy sauce, and sherry. Add water and simmer 1 minute. Add red roast pork and onions and stir ½ minute. Serves 3.

The taofu, instead of being sautéed, may be deep fried in 3 cups oil.

ROAST PORK AND TAOFU

叉
燒
豆
付

1 cup cubed roast pork
4 cups cubed taofu
6 tablespoons oil
¼ cup green onions, cut in
  ¼-inch lengths

½ cup cubed red peppers
2 tablespoons soy sauce
1 tablespoon sherry
1 tablespoon gourmet powder
½ cup water

Heat pan, add oil, and fry taofu until light brown. Add pork, green onions, and peppers. Mix well and add soy sauce, sherry, gourmet powder, and water. Simmer 2 minutes. Serves 4.

SHERRY PORK

酒
炒
肉

1 cup sliced pork
2 tablespoons oil
2 cloves garlic, crushed
¼ cup green onions, cut in
  2-inch lengths

¼ cup crushed fresh ginger
½ cup sherry
1 tablespoon sugar
1 teaspoon salt

Heat pan, add oil, and sauté garlic and onions 2 seconds. Add pork and sauté 3 seconds. Add ginger, sherry, sugar, and salt. Cook 1½ minutes. Serves 2.

SOY SAUCE PORK AND EGGS

豉
油
肉
絲
蛋

12-ounce piece of belly pork
2 tablespoons oil
3 cloves garlic, crushed
¼ cup green onions, cut in
  1-inch lengths

4 tablespoons sherry
½ cup soy sauce
1½ tablespoons sugar
7 hard-boiled eggs, shelled
1½ cups water

Cut pork into 1-inch strips and bring to a boil in 2 cups of water. Continue boiling 2 minutes. Heat pan, add oil, and sauté garlic and pork 1 minute. Add green onions, sherry, soy sauce, sugar, hard-boiled eggs, and water. Simmer until pork is tender (about 50 minutes). Serves 3.

SPARERIBS AND PICKLED VEGETABLES

甜
酸
排
骨

1¼ pounds spareribs
2 cups oil

2 teaspoons cornstarch
1 tablespoon soy sauce

Have butcher cut spareribs into 2-inch pieces. Bring spareribs to a boil in 1½ cups water and simmer until tender. Remove to plate and rub with mixture of cornstarch and soy sauce. Heat pan, add oil, and fry spareribs until light brown. Remove, drain, and arrange on platter.

SAUCE

½ onion, sliced
½ cup sliced pickled vegetables
    (canned)
1 cup pickled vegetable juice
3 tablespoons vinegar

1 tablespoon cornstarch
¼ cup sugar
1 teaspoon sherry
1 tablespoon soy sauce

Heat pan, add 2 tablespoons oil, and sauté onion 2 seconds. Mix pickled vegetable juice, vinegar, cornstarch, sugar, sherry, and soy sauce and add to onion. Bring to a boil. Add pickled vegetables and simmer 1 minute. Pour over spareribs. Serves 4.

SPRING ROLLS (EGG ROLLS)

春
卷

½ pound lean pork, shredded
½ pound bean sprouts
8 large dried mushrooms
3¼ cups oil
2 stalks celery, sliced
20 flour doilies, 5 x 5 inches

MIX: 3 tablespoons soy sauce
2 teaspoons sherry
1 teaspoon gourmet
    powder
1 teaspoon salt
MIX: 2 teaspoons cornstarch
4 tablespoons water

Marinate pork in mixture of soy sauce, sherry, gourmet powder, and salt. Drop bean sprouts in boiling water for 1 second and remove. Soak dried mushrooms and clean (page 21). Squeeze dry and slice. Heat pan, add 2 tablespoons oil, and sauté celery and bean sprouts 1 minute. Remove. Reheat pan, add 2 tablespoons oil, and sauté pork and mushrooms 1 minute. Add sautéed celery and bean sprouts and stir 2 minutes. When cool spread 1½ tablespoons of mixture on each doily. Fold both edges about ½ inch, moisten with cornstarch mixture, and roll. Heat 3 cups oil and deep fry rolls until light brown.

The flour doilies may be bought at a Chinese bakery. Instead of doilies pork caul may be used (as in Duck Liver Rolls, page 79), or Egg Noodle dough (page 128) rolled paper thin and cut into doilies 4 x 6 inches. Sliced bamboo shoots may be substituted for celery. Red roast pork may be substituted for raw pork.

STEAMED HIND LEG OF PORK

蒸
肘
子

2 pounds pork hind leg
6 tablespoons soy sauce
4 tablespoons oil
6 buttons garlic, crushed
1 teaspoon salt
1 square piece red bean curd
2 tablespoons sugar
1 anise
1 tablespoon sugar

3 tablespoons sherry
4 tablespoons chicken stock
2 tablespoons Ti Chu Yu
    (Thick Cantonese Sauce)
1 bunch spinach, cut in 2-inch
    lengths
2 tablespoons cornstarch
MIX: 2 tablespoons cornstarch
    1 cup water

Wash pork and prick skin with pointed knife or ice pick until it is well covered with holes. Rub with 2 tablespoons soy sauce. Bring to a boil in 2 cups of water and continue boiling until the skin is brown (about 30 minutes). Remove to a bowl of cold water and let stand 20 minutes. Remove. Heat pan, add oil, and sauté garlic until brown. Add pork and brown well. Add salt, red bean curd, remainder of soy sauce, and sugar. Sauté 1 minute. Add mixture of cornstarch and water and simmer 2 minutes. Remove pork and gravy to deep bowl and put anise on top. Add sugar, sherry, chicken stock, and Ti Chu Yu. Steam 1½ hours until tender. Remove anise.

Drop spinach in boiling water and cook 5 minutes. Remove and drain. Arrange on large platter. Place pork on spinach. Add 2 tablespoons cornstarch to gravy and bring to a boil. Pour over pork. Serves 4.

STEAMED RED PORK AND POTATOES

扣
肉

Belly pork is made up of alternate layers of lean and fat. This dish, served with steamed buns at the end of a birthday or wedding feast, is a reminder that life is made up of lean and fat years.

12-ounce piece of belly pork
2 tablespoons oil
4 small cloves garlic, chopped
1 small piece ginger, chopped
3 tablespoons soy sauce
2 tablespoons sugar

½ teaspoon salt
⅓ cup preserved red bean curd
2 teaspoons red coloring
1 teaspoon 5-spice
3 medium-sized potatoes

Bring pork to a boil in 2 cups water and continue boiling 10 minutes. Remove. Heat pan, add oil, and fry garlic and ginger until brown. Add pork and brown on all sides. Add soy sauce, sugar, and salt. Sauté 1 minute. Add bean curd, red coloring, and 5-spice. Sauté 1 minute. Remove, saving the sauce. When pork is cool cut into strips 1 inch wide and rub each strip with the sauce. Cut potatoes into ¼-inch thick slices. Arrange alternate rows of pork and potatoes in a bowl and add any left-over sauce. Steam 1 hour. Serves 5.

STEWED SPARERIBS AND TURNIPS

蘿
蔔
蒸
排
骨

¾ pound spareribs
1 large turnip
2 tablespoons oil
1 tablespoon crushed garlic
2 tablespoons chopped onion
2 tablespoons preserved Chinese
    black beans

2 tablespoons preserved red
    bean curd
3 tablespoons soy sauce
1 tablespoon sugar
1½ cups water

Have butcher cut spareribs into 2-inch pieces. Peel turnip, cut in two lengthwise, and cut into ¼-inch thick slices. Heat pan, add oil, and sauté garlic and onion 2 seconds. Add spareribs and sauté 1 minute. Add preserved black beans, red bean curd, soy sauce, and sugar and sauté 3 seconds. Add water and simmer 15 minutes. Add sliced turnip and simmer 10 minutes. Serves 4.

SWEET-SOUR PIG'S SHANKS

酸
猪
脚

1 pig foreshank (2¾ pounds)
4 tablespoons oil
6 cloves garlic, crushed
3 tablespoons soy sauce

¾ cup brown sugar
½ cup crushed fresh ginger
3 cups vinegar
½ cup water

Have butcher cut foreshank into 2-inch pieces. Heat pan, add oil, and brown garlic. Add pieces of foreshank and brown slightly for 2 minutes. Add soy sauce, brown sugar, and ginger. Sauté 2 minutes. Add vinegar and water and simmer 1½ hours. Serves 4.

The following variation of this recipe is served to convalescing mothers beginning the third day after the baby is born and continuing until the end of the first month.

2 pig foreshanks
3 cups black Chinese vinegar
1 cup cider vinegar

8 slabs Chinese brown sugar
1¼ cups crushed fresh ginger

Have the butcher cut the foreshanks into 3-inch pieces. Bring foreshanks to a boil, simmer 20 minutes, and drain. Add black vinegar, cider vinegar, brown sugar and ginger. Simmer 1½ hours.

VEGETABLES

栄
類

Many a Westerner who has never liked vegetables is surprised and delighted with those cooked Chinese style. Since the Chinese like their vegetables bright, crisp, and barely done, they usually cook them a very short time over high heat, either in their own juices or in small amounts of oil or water. This brief cooking requires that they be young and tender and fresh from the garden. Nutritionists now agree that this method helps to keep food values intact.

Water cress, spinach, lettuce, and other soft and watery vegetables are often sautéed in a little oil with no other liquid than their own juices. Harder vegetables are often parboiled a minute or two, then combined with other ingredients for final cooking.

The Chinese farmer produces practically all of the varieties of vegetables known in the West, plus many others. Those not raised extensively or at all in the West are, however, gradually appearing in American markets, either fresh or canned.

Some of the less common vegetables which help to give Chinese cooking its distinctive taste and texture include water chestnuts, bamboo shoots, bean and pea sprouts, lotus root, Chinese mushrooms and bitter melon. All of these may be bought at Chinese groceries in their fresh state, but water chestnuts and bamboo shoots are also canned and the mushrooms are usually dried.

Always under the threat of food shortage, the Chinese farmer must use every possible area or method to preserve or increase the supply. Vegetables not consumed when they are in season are preserved by drying, salting, or pickling. Seeds and even flower petals are dried and used as food. If a farmer has a stream or pond he raises not only crabs and fish but water chestnuts, lotus plants, and other vegetables. In his house he keeps beans and peas on racks in a warm, damp place so he can have fresh sprouts without using precious land space, and today the practice of raising vegetables in hothouses during the long winter months is fairly common.

Occidentals think of the Chinese diet as consisting mainly of rice and vegetables, and with good reason. The scarcity of meat in China has forced cooks to develop hundreds of recipes using large amounts of vegetables, with only enough meat, fish, or poultry to flavor them.

The Chinese connect the eating of meat with man's animal nature and think of a vegetable diet as more spiritual than one including meat. Consequently many beliefs and religious customs have grown up around vegetable dishes. Some holy men and philosophers live entirely on vegetables and rice, some through conviction, others because of the high cost of meat. It is customary that the first meal of the New Year be completely vegetarian. The *Analects* report that Confucius, after hearing some beautiful music, was so uplifted that "for three months he did not know the taste of flesh."

On the birthday of the Buddha, the eighth day of the fourth month, some devout Buddhists set several pints of green and yellow beans in bowls before them. They then transfer the beans from one bowl to another, repeating the name of the Buddha as each is transferred, much as a Christian tells beads of a rosary. The beans are then cooked with a little salt and given to passers-by.

Cooked vegetables may be made more attractive by garnishing them with cashew nuts, or walnuts or almonds which have been shelled, blanched, peeled, and fried in deep fat until light brown.

ASPARAGUS WITH CHICKEN BROTH

露
笋
鷄
湯

108

16 stalks canned asparagus
½ cup chicken broth
2 tablespoons oil
1 tablespoon sherry

½ teaspoon salt
2 tablespoons soy sauce
MIX: 1 tablespoon cornstarch
1 teaspoon water

Heat pan and add oil. Add chicken broth, sherry, salt, soy sauce, and mixture of cornstarch and water. Stir 1 minute. Add asparagus and simmer 3½ minutes. Serves 4.

BAMBOO SHOOTS AND CHINESE PEAS

竹
笋
青
豆

2 cups shredded bamboo shoots
2 cups Chinese peas
¼ pound sirloin tip, sliced
1 teaspoon salt
1 teaspoon cornstarch

2 teaspoons sherry
1 tablespoon soy sauce
1 teaspoon sugar
8 tablespoons oil
¼ cup water

Remove ends and strings from Chinese peas. Drop into 2 cups of boiling water for 3 seconds and remove. Add salt, cornstarch, sherry, soy sauce, and sugar to beef. Heat pan, add 6 tablespoons oil, and sauté bamboo shoots 1 minute. Remove and pour off oil. Reheat pan, add 2 tablespoons oil, and sauté beef ½ minute. Add bamboo shoots, Chinese peas, and water. Stir 2 minutes. Serves 4.

Chinese peas are also known as "snow peas."

BAMBOO SHOOTS AND MUSHROOMS

冬
菇
竹
笋

3 cups sliced bamboo shoots
11 dried mushrooms
10 tablespoons oil
2 teaspoons sugar

1 tablespoon sherry
3 tablespoons soy sauce
½ cup water

Soak mushrooms and remove stems (page 21). Squeeze dry and slice. Heat pan, add 8 tablespoons oil, and sauté bamboo shoots 1 minute. Remove and pour off oil. Reheat pan, add 2 tablespoons oil, and sauté mushrooms 2 minutes. Add bamboo shoots, sugar, sherry, soy sauce, and water. Simmer 2 minutes. Serves 4.

One 7-ounce can of mushrooms may be used instead of dried mushrooms.

BEAN SPROUTS AND CARROTS

金
笋
錢
芽

5 cups bean sprouts
¾ cup shredded carrots
4 tablespoons oil
¼ cup water
¼ cup green onions, cut in
    2-inch lengths

MIX: 1 teaspoon cornstarch
½ teaspoon salt
2 teaspoons
    Worcestershire Sauce
1 tablespoon soy sauce

Drop bean sprouts into 2 cups boiling water and let stand 2 seconds. Remove. Reheat water to boiling and parboil carrots 1 minute. Remove. Heat pan, add oil, and sauté bean sprouts and carrots ½ minute. Add ¼ cup water and mixture of cornstarch, salt, Worcestershire Sauce, and soy sauce. Add green onions and simmer 1 minute, stirring constantly. Serves 4.

BEAN SPROUTS AND DRIED TAOFU

豆
付
炒
芽
菜

12 ounces bean sprouts
4 pieces Chinese dried taofu
  (1 inch square)
¼ cup green onions, cut in
  1-inch lengths
3 tablespoons oil
¼ cup cashew nuts

MIX: ½ teaspoon salt
Few grains pepper
2 tablespoons oyster sauce
1 tablespoon soy sauce
3 tablespoons water

Cut each piece of taofu in two. Heat pan, add oil, and sauté taofu 2 seconds. Stir in bean sprouts and green onions and sauté 3 seconds. Add mixture of salt, pepper, oyster sauce, soy sauce and water. Mix well and cook 1½ minutes. Remove to bowl and garnish with cashew nuts. Serves 4.

The secret of this dish is not to overcook the bean sprouts.

BEAN SPROUTS AND PORK

芽
菜
炒
猪
肉

4¼ cups bean sprouts
½ cup sliced pork
½ cup water
4 tablespoons oil

MIX: 1 teaspoon cornstarch
2 teaspoons sugar
½ teaspoon salt
2 tablespoons soy sauce
1 tablespoon sherry

Marinate pork in mixture of cornstarch, sugar, salt, soy sauce, and sherry. Heat pan, add oil, and sauté bean sprouts 1 minute. Remove. Reheat pan, add 2 tablespoons oil, and sauté pork 1 minute. Add bean sprouts and water and cook 1 minute. Serves 4.

BEAN SPROUTS AND ROAST DUCK

芽
菜
炒
燒
鴨

½ pound bean sprouts
2 tablespoons oil
½ pound roast duck, shredded
½ teaspoon salt

1 tablespoon sherry
2 teaspoons soy sauce
2 tablespoons water

Drop bean sprouts into boiling water for 1 second. Remove. Heat pan, add oil, and sauté bean sprouts 2 seconds. Add duck, salt, sherry, soy sauce, and water. Cook ½ minute, stirring constantly. Serves 3. Oyster sauce may be substituted for soy sauce.

BITTER MELON STUFFED WITH PORK

6 medium-sized bitter melons
8 water chestnuts
½ cup green onions, cut in
  ¼-inch lengths
1½ cups ground roast pork

1 tablespoon sherry
3 tablespoons soy sauce
¼ teaspoon pepper
½ teaspoon gourmet powder

醸
苦
瓜

Cut each melon crosswise into 1½-inch pieces and remove the seeds. Peel water chestnuts and mince. Add water chestnuts and green onions to roast pork. Add sherry, soy sauce, pepper, and gourmet powder and mix well. Stuff each piece of melon with the meat filling.

SAUCE

1½ cups water
2 tablespoons cornstarch
1 tablespoon sherry

2 tablespoons soy sauce
1 teaspoon salt
1 teaspoon gourmet powder

Mix all ingredients and bring to a boil. Lower the heat until the sauce is simmering gently, then add the stuffed melon. Cover and simmer 30 minutes. Serves 6.

BROCCOLI

芥
蘭

1 pound broccoli
½ teaspoon salt
4 tablespoons oil

MIX: 2 tablespoons oyster sauce
1 teaspoon sugar
⅓ cup broccoli water

Wash broccoli, peel stems, and slice diagonally. Bring 2 cups of water to a boil, add salt and broccoli, and simmer 1½ minutes. Drain, saving ⅓ cup water. Heat pan, add oil, and sauté broccoli 1 minute. Add mixture of broccoli water, oyster sauce, and sugar. Stir well 4 seconds. Serves 3.

CAULIFLOWER AND HAM

椰
菜
花
炒
火
腿

¾ pound cauliflower
⅓ cup sliced raw ham
3 tablespoons oil
2 tablespoons soy sauce
1 tablespoon sherry

½ teaspoon salt
½ cup cauliflower water
MIX: 1 tablespoon water
2 teaspoons cornstarch

Break cauliflower into flowerets and cut each floweret in two lengthwise. Drop in boiling water and parboil 1½ minutes. Save ½ cup of cauliflower water. Heat pan, add oil, and sauté ham ½ minute. Add cauliflower, cauliflower water, soy sauce, sherry, salt, and cornstarch mixed with water. Sauté 1½ minutes. Serves 3.

CAULIFLOWER, WATER CHESTNUTS, AND MUSHROOMS

½ pound cauliflower
6 water chestnuts
5 dried mushrooms
3 tablespoons oil
½ cup mushroom water
¼ cup chicken stock

1 teaspoon sherry
2 tablespoons soy sauce
1 teaspoon salt
2 teaspoons cornstarch
1 teaspoon sesame oil

榮
花
馬
蹄
冬
菇

Break cauliflower into flowerets and cut each floweret in two lengthwise. Drop into 2 cups boiling water and parboil 1½ minutes. Peel water chestnuts and slice. Soak mushrooms and clean (page 21). Squeeze dry and slice. (Save ½ cup of second water.) Heat pan, add oil, and sauté water chestnuts and mushrooms 1 minute. Add mushroom water, chicken stock, sherry, soy sauce, salt, cornstarch, and sesame oil. Simmer ½ minute. Add cauliflower and simmer 1 minute. Serves 4.

A 7-ounce can of mushrooms may be substituted for dried mushrooms.

CHINESE WHITE STEM CABBAGE

白
菜

1 bunch Chinese white cabbage
½ pound fresh shrimps
2 tablespoons oil
½ teaspoon salt

2 teaspoons soy sauce
1 teaspoon gourmet powder
¼ cup water

Wash cabbage and cut off about 3 inches of the top, leaving about 4 inches of green for color. Cut stalks into 2-inch lengths. Drop cabbage into 2 cups of boiling water and let stand 1 minute. Remove. Clean shrimps and cut each diagonally into 3 pieces. Heat pan, add oil, and sauté shrimps 4 seconds. Add cabbage, salt, soy sauce, gourmet powder, and water. Simmer 1 minute. Serves 3.

CUCUMBERS

黃
瓜

2 cucumbers (1½ pounds)
1 tablespoon cornstarch
2 tablespoons soy sauce
½ teaspoon salt

2 teaspoons sesame seeds
1 teaspoon gourmet powder
2 cups water
2 teaspoons oil

Peel cucumbers and cut lengthwise into halves. Combine all other ingredients and bring to a boil. Add cucumbers and simmer 15 minutes. Serves 4.

CUCUMBERS AND LONG RICE

黃
瓜
粉
絲

3 medium-sized cucumbers
½ bunch long rice

MIX: 1 cup chicken stock
1 teaspoon soy sauce
¼ teaspoon salt
2 teaspoons cornstarch

Peel cucumbers and cut crosswise into ½-inch slices. Soak long rice 10 minutes in 2 cups warm water. Drain. Bring mixture of chicken stock, soy sauce, salt, and cornstarch to a boil, add cucumbers and long rice, and simmer 10 minutes. Serves 3.

LEEKS AND BAMBOO SHOOTS

韭
菜
竹
笋

1 cup leeks, cut in 2-inch
    lengths
1 cup finely sliced bamboo
    shoots
½ pound pork, sliced
3 tablespoons oil
½ cup water

MIX: 1 teaspoon cornstarch
½ teaspoon salt
1 tablespoon soy sauce
1 teaspoon sherry

Marinate pork in mixture of cornstarch, salt, soy sauce, and sherry. Heat pan, add oil, and sauté pork 1 minute. Add bamboo shoots and leeks and sauté 1½ minutes. Add water and heat through. Serves 3.

MONK'S FOOD

羅
漢
齋

12 dried lotus seeds
6 dried mushrooms
8 water chestnuts
1 bunch Chinese long rice
1 cup dried seaweed
4 tablespoons oil
1 cup chestnuts, shelled
2 bamboo shoots, sliced

½ pound bean sprouts
1 cup sliced celery cabbage
3 cups chicken stock
3 tablespoons soy sauce
½ teaspoon salt
2 teaspoons sherry
1 teaspoon cornstarch
½ cup red bean curd

Soak lotus seeds in 1 cup water 40 minutes. Bring to a boil and simmer 8 minutes. Remove and peel covering from seeds. Soak mushrooms and clean (page 21). Peel water chestnuts and slice. Soak long rice in 2 cups water 15 minutes. Remove and cut in 5-inch lengths. Wash seaweed and soak in 3 cups hot water 20 minutes. Remove and wash thoroughly. Heat pan, add oil, and sauté lotus seeds, mushrooms, water chestnuts, long rice, seaweed, chestnuts, bamboo shoots, bean sprouts, and celery cabbage 2 minutes. Add chicken stock, soy sauce, salt, sherry, cornstarch, and bean curd. Simmer until vegetables are cooked. Serves 6.

Fried taofu (4 pieces 1 inch square cut in two), ½ cup fungi (see directions for soaking, page 21), and ½ cup shelled and peeled gingko nuts may also be added if desired.

MUSHROOMS AND SPINACH

波
菜
冬
菇

1 bunch spinach
14 dried mushrooms
3 tablespoons oil
3 tablespoons soy sauce
1 tablespoon sugar
1 tablespoon sherry

½ teaspoon salt
1 cup water
½ cup mushroom water
MIX: 1 teaspoon cornstarch
1 teaspoon water

Soak mushrooms (page 21), clean, and squeeze dry. Save ½ cup of the second water. Heat pan, add oil, and sauté mushrooms 1 minute. Add soy sauce, sugar, sherry, and salt. Sauté ½ minute. Add water and mushroom water and simmer 12 minutes. Wash spinach and cut in 2-inch lengths. Drop spinach in 1 cup boiling water, parboil 1 minute, and remove to platter. Add cornstarch paste to mushroom sauce and simmer ½ minute. Pour over spinach. Serves 3.

One 7-ounce can of button mushrooms may be substituted for dried mushrooms.

MUSHROOMS AND WATER CHESTNUTS

冬
菇
馬
蹄

28 dried mushrooms
15 water chestnuts
2 tablespoons oil
1 tablespoon sherry

1 tablespoon sugar
½ teaspoon salt
1 tablespoon soy sauce
¾ cup chicken broth

Soak mushrooms and remove stems (page 21). Squeeze dry and slice. Peel water chestnuts and cut each into 4 slices. Heat pan, and add oil. Add mushrooms, sherry, sugar, salt, and soy sauce and sauté 2 minutes. Add water chestnuts and chicken broth and simmer 12 minutes or until mushrooms are tender. Serves 3.

A 13-ounce can of whole mushrooms may be used instead of dried mushrooms, in which case substitute mushroom liquor for chicken broth.

PICKLED CUCUMBERS

黃
瓜
酸

2 medium-sized cucumbers
2 teaspoons salt
½ cup vinegar

5 tablespoons sugar
2 teaspoons fresh ginger juice
1 teaspoon sesame seeds

Peel cucumbers, leaving four green strips. Cut in two lengthwise, remove seeds, and slice fine. Place in bowl, add salt, and let stand 10 minutes. Squeeze off excess water and pack in sterilized quart jar. Mix vinegar, sugar, ginger juice, and sesame seeds. Bring to a boil. Pour over sliced cucumbers, let cool, and cover. Serve cold as pickles or as a garnish for spareribs.

PICKLED MUSTARD CABBAGE

咸
酸
菜

5 cups mustard cabbage stalks,
   cut in 1-inch lengths
2 tablespoons salt

2 cups vinegar
¾ cup sugar

Bring water to a boil and add salt. Drop mustard cabbage into boiling water and parboil uncovered 1 minute. Drain. Mix vinegar and sugar and bring to a boil. Pour over mustard cabbage. Pour into hot sterilized glasses and seal.

Two tablespoons chopped ginger or 2 teaspoons ginger juice may be added to vinegar and sugar when boiling.

PICKLED TURNIPS

酸
蘿
蔔

2 cups sliced turnips
2 tablespoons salt
1 cup vinegar

¾ cup sugar
¼ teaspoon paprika
½ teaspoon yellow coloring

Peel turnips and cut crosswise into thin slices. Add salt, mix well, and let stand 30 minutes. Drain off excess moisture. Mix vinegar, sugar, paprika, and coloring in saucepan and bring to a boil. Drop turnip slices in boiling mixture and simmer 1 minute. Pour into sterilized glass jars and seal.

SALTED TURNIPS

咸
菜
寶

4 medium-size turnips

2 cups Bean Sauce

Wash turnips but do not peel. Cut crosswise into slices 1 inch thick. Pour Bean Sauce into large bowl, add sliced turnips, and let stand 3 days.

SALTED TARO BALLS

炸
廣
東
玉
頭

2 pounds taro
2 tablespoons mochi flour
2 tablespoons rice flour

1 teaspoon salt
¼ teaspoon pepper
4 cups oil

Peel taro, wash, and wipe dry. Cut crosswise into 1-inch pieces, slice diagonally, and cut each slice into thin strips. Sift together mochi flour, rice flour, salt, and pepper. Sprinkle evenly over shredded taro. Form into small balls. Heat oil and deep fry until brown and crisp.

Salted Taro Balls are served during New Year's festivals and with afternoon tea.

SPINACH

波
菜

1 bunch spinach
3 tablespoons oil
2 cloves garlic, chopped
1 teaspoon fresh ginger

1 teaspoon soy sauce
1 teaspoon salt
½ cup water

Wash spinach, cut off 2 inches of the stem, and cut the rest into 3-inch lengths. Heat pan, add oil, and sauté garlic and ginger 2 seconds. Add spinach, soy sauce, salt, and water. Mix well and simmer 5 minutes. Serves 4.

STUFFED BELL PEPPERS

釀
辣
椒

7 medium-sized bell peppers
10 water chestnuts
¼ cup green onions, cut in
   ¼-inch lengths
1 cup ground pork
1 tablespoon sherry

1 teaspoon cornstarch
1 teaspoon gourmet powder
½ teaspoon salt
3 tablespoons soy sauce
1 teaspoon sugar
1 tablespoon oil

Cut bell peppers into halves crosswise. Bring to a boil in 3 cups of water and simmer 5 minutes. Remove, drain, and take out seeds. Peel water chestnuts and chop. Add water chestnuts, green onions, sherry, cornstarch, gourmet powder, salt, soy sauce, sugar, and oil to pork and mix well. Stuff each half pepper with mixture. Arrange in large bowl and steam 40 minutes. Serves 4.

A medium-sized onion, chopped, may be substituted for water chestnuts and 1 cup fish cake for pork.

STUFFED EGGPLANT

釀
茄
子

1 large eggplant
8 water chestnuts
¾ pound ground pork
1 small onion, minced
1 tablespoon minced fresh
   ginger

1 tablespoon sherry
2 teaspoons soy sauce
½ teaspoon salt
1 teaspoon sugar

Peel water chestnuts and mince. Combine water chestnuts, pork, onion, and ginger. Add sherry, soy sauce, salt, and sugar. Mix well. Wash and peel egg plant and cut in two lengthwise. Remove seeds. Stuff each half with mixture. Steam 30 minutes. Serves 2.

Beef may be substituted for pork.

STUFFED MUSHROOMS

14 medium-sized dried
    mushrooms
6 water chestnuts
½ pound ground pork
½ cup minced cooked ham
½ teaspoon salt

½ tablespoon cornstarch
2 tablespoons soy sauce
1 egg white
1 tablespoon sugar
1 tablespoon sherry
3 tablespoons oil

Soak mushrooms and remove stems (page 21). Peel water chestnuts and mince. Combine water chestnuts, pork, and ham. Add salt, cornstarch, and 1 tablespoon soy sauce. Add egg white and mix well. Heat pan, add oil, and sauté whole mushrooms 2 minutes. Add sugar, sherry, and 1 tablespoon soy sauce and sauté 1 minute. Remove to deep plate or bowl. Stuff by packing 1½ tablespoons of the pork mixture inside each inverted mushroom. Steam 30 minutes. Add 2 tablespoons hot chicken stock. Serves 4.

Fresh mushrooms may be used instead of dried ones. One cup fish cake may be used instead of pork and ham.

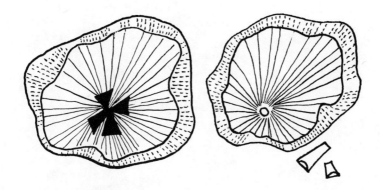

SWAMP CABBAGE

1 bunch swamp cabbage
2 tablespoons oil
3 gloves garlic, crushed
3 tablespoons soy bean cake

2 slices fresh ginger
1 teaspoon sugar
1 teaspoon salt
¼ cup water

Wash cabbage well and cut about 3 inches off the stems. Cut the rest in 2-inch lengths. Heat pan, add oil, and sauté garlic and bean cake 3 seconds. Add swamp cabbage and ginger and stir well. Cook 2 minutes. Add sugar, salt, and water. Stir well 1 minute. Serves 4.

WHITE FIGS

白
無
花
菓

16 medium-sized white figs
1½ cups chicken stock
1 tablespoon cornstarch
2 teaspoons soy sauce

1 teaspoon sherry
½ teaspoon salt
¼ cup shredded green onions

Wash figs and remove stems. Combine chicken stock, cornstarch, soy sauce, sherry, and salt. Bring to a boil, add figs, and simmer over medium heat 20 minutes. Add green onions and simmer 2 minutes. Serves 4.

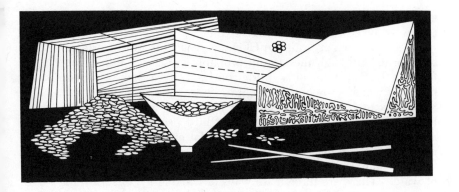

RICE

飯
類

Rice and noodles are to the Orient what bread is to the Occident. Rice is the basic sustainer of human life throughout most of China, although wheat is the staple of the north. A bowl of rice symbolizes all food in Chinese literature. According to a Chinese proverb, a dinner without rice is like a pretty girl with only one eye. The accidental overturning of a bowl of rice presages misfortune. Doing it deliberatly is as much of an insult as spitting on a doorstep is in Italy. When a man quits his job, he has "broken his rice bowl." A servant receiving board and room but no wages is working for "only a bowl of rice." In China one does not ask the "sixty-four dollar question," one asks the "rice-bowl question."

The cultivation of rice in China was close to its present state of development when history was first written on bones and stones. The rice fields as seen in the deltas and terraced valleys of South China today are shallow swamps from which billions of green spears point to the sky. Low dikes separate individual fields. Ungainly water buffaloes plod through the mud, pulling the ploughs. In places where there is not enough fodder to sustain buffaloes, ploughs are pulled by men.

Many of the present customs of China have developed out of ancient rites. In the almost forgotten past the Chinese celebrated thanksgiving for bounteous harvests by offering sacrifices to the five household gods, who were in charge of the door, the main gate, the kitchen stove, the center of the house where water from the roof was collected, and the well. A surviving rite is the making of a rice and fruit gruel at daybreak on the eighth day of the twelfth month and presenting it to ancestors and friends as a gesture of thanksgiving. This gruel is to their celebration what turkey is to the American Thanksgiving.

Rice is thrown at brides in China as well as in other parts of the world. Although the custom probably arose as a prayer for fertility, legend tells of a bride pursued by a huge golden pheasant which a sorcerer had sent to destroy her. She outwitted the pheasant by ordering that rice be thrown out of the door before she appeared. While the great bird pecked away at the rice she stepped safely into her red bridal chair and was borne away to her wedding.

Rice should always be washed thoroughly in several changes of water. There are three main ways of cooking it. First, a thin soup, or "congee," is made by boiling a little rice in a great deal of water. This is usually eaten for breakfast with salted eggs and other highly flavored foods, or as a late evening snack. When served as a snack, bits of beef, chicken, pork, or sliced raw fish are added to give it flavor. Second, a thicker soup, or chowder, is made by boiling the rice in less water and adding other ingredients. Since this gives the greatest bulk for the least amount of rice it is a common dish among the poor. Third, the usual boiled or steamed rice is made by using even less water and cooking it until all moisture has evaporated. The amount of water used depends on personal preference, but the general rule is that the water level should be one inch above the rice level in the pot.

In addition to the ordinary rice there is glutinous or mochi rice, which is used mostly for festival dishes and fancy pastries.

BEEF RICE CHOWDER

牛
肉
粥

2 pounds beef bones	14 cups water
1 pound ground beef	3 tablespoons soy sauce
1 cup rice	2 teaspoons salt
½ cup green onions, shredded	

Bring soup bones and water to a boil and simmer 1 hour. Remove bones. Wash rice thoroughly. Add beef and rice to beef stock and simmer 50 minutes. Add green onions, soy sauce, and salt. Serves 4.

BOILED RICE I

保
飯

Wash rice in cold water 3 times. Add 1 cup water for each cup of rice. Bring to a boil in a covered pot and continue boiling over medium flame until water has evaporated. Reduce to low heat and let steam 20 minutes.

Do not stir rice while boiling, otherwise it will not stand out in separate grains. If it is cooked on a gas stove turn the flame low after the water has evaporated.

BOILED RICE II

保
飯

2 cups rice
2 cups water

Wash rice 3 times. Add water, cover, and cook over high heat 3 minutes. Turn to low heat and simmer 17 minutes.

BOILED RICE AND BEEF

牛
肉
飯

2 cups rice
½ pound sirloin tip
   sliced very thin
8 dried mushrooms
2 tablespoons oil
4 tablespoons oyster sauce

½ teaspoon salt
2½ cups water
MIX: 2 teaspoons soy sauce
   ½ teaspoon sugar
   4 tablespoons water

Soak mushrooms and clean (page 21). Squeeze dry and slice. Heat pan, add oil, and sauté sliced mushrooms 1 minute. Add mixture of soy sauce, sugar, and water. Sauté ½ minute and remove to bowl. Add thinly sliced sirloin tip, oyster sauce, and salt. Mix well.

Wash rice several times and drain. Add water, cover, and bring to a boil. Cook over medium heat until the water has boiled off. Place the beef mixture on top of the rice, cover, and cook over low heat 15 minutes. Mix thoroughly. Serves 3.

BOILED RICE AND CHINESE SAUSAGES

2 cups rice
2 cups water
4 Chinese sausages

Wash sausages in warm water. Slice diagonally very thin. Wash rice 3 times. Add water, cover and cook over medium heat. When the water has evaporated, stir the slices of sausage into the cooked rice. Steam over low heat 25 minutes. Serves 3.

121

BOILED RICE WITH CHICKEN AND SAUSAGES

臘
腸
鷄
飯

2½ cups rice
1 fryer (3 pounds)
5 Chinese sausages
3 cups water

1 tablespoon soy sauce
½ teaspoon salt
2 tablespoons oyster sauce

Wash rice 4 times. Cut chicken into segments (page 62). Cut each sausage into 6 pieces. Put rice in pot, add water, and allow to boil 3 minutes. Add chicken and sausages and simmer until the water is evaporated. Steam over low heat 45 minutes. Remove chicken and sausages to separate platter and add oyster sauce. The rice will have absorbed a delicious flavor from the chicken and sausages.

If the rice, chicken, and sausages are served as one dish omit the oyster sauce.

CHICKEN RICE CHOWDER

鷄
粥

1 fryer (3 pounds)
26 cups water
3 tablespoons soy sauce
1 teaspoon salt

1 tablespoon sesame oil
3 cups rice
2 ch'ung choy
¼ cup green onions, shredded

Wash chicken and put in deep pot. Add 20 cups water and bring to a boil. Continue boiling 20 minutes, then lower the heat and simmer 1 hour. Remove chicken from broth. When cool remove meat from bones and shred. Add soy sauce, salt, and sesame oil to shredded chicken.

Wash ch'ung choy and shred. Wash rice thoroughly and add to chicken broth. Add 6 cups of water, bring to a boil, and simmer 30 minutes. Add chicken, ch'ung choy, and onions. Serves 8.

FRIED RICE AND CHICKEN

鷄
炒
飯

4 cups cooked rice
1 cup diced chicken breast meat
4 tablespoons oil
½ cup diced mushrooms
    (canned)

½ teaspoon salt
2 tablespoons soy sauce
½ cup green onions, cut in
    ¼-inch lengths
3 medium-sized eggs, beaten

Heat pan, add oil, and sauté chicken and mushrooms 1 minute. Add rice, salt, and soy sauce, and sauté 2 minutes. Add green onions and stir ½ minute. Add eggs, mix well, and sauté 1 minute. Serves 6.

122

FRIED RICE AND CRABMEAT

蟹
炒
飯

4 cups cooked rice	2 large eggs, beaten
5 tablespoons oil	1 tablespoon soy sauce
1 cup shredded onions	¾ teaspoon salt
1 can crabmeat, shredded	½ cup chopped green onions

Heat pan, add oil, and fry onions 1 minute. Add rice and fry 1 minute, stirring constantly. Add crabmeat, eggs, soy sauce, salt, and green onions. Mix well and serve. Serves 6.

FRIED RICE AND HAM

火
腿
炒
飯

4 cups cooked rice	½ cup green onions, cut in
½ cup shredded cooked ham	½-inch lengths
4 tablespoons oil	1 tablespoon soy sauce
1 large onion, shredded	½ teaspoon salt
2 eggs, beaten	Parsley

Heat pan, add oil, and fry onion ½ minute. Add rice and sauté 1 minute. Add eggs, ham, green onions, soy sauce, and salt. Sauté 1 minute. Remove to platter and garnish with parsley.

FRIED RICE AND LOBSTER

龍
蝦
炒
飯

2 cups cooked rice	¼ cup green onions, cut in
¾ cup lobster (canned)	¼-inch lengths
3 tablespoons oil	1 large egg, beaten
¼ cup diced bamboo shoot	2 tablespoons soy sauce
¼ cup diced mushrooms	
(canned)	

Heat pan, add oil, and sauté bamboo shoot and mushrooms 1 minute. Add rice and sauté 1 minute. Add green onions and egg and mix well. Add lobster and soy sauce. Stir 1 minute. Serves 3.

Dried mushrooms may be used instead of canned. See instructions for soaking and cleaning, page 21.

FRIED RICE AND ROAST PORK

叉
燒
炒
飯

4 cups cooked rice	¼ cup green onions, cut in
1 cup diced roast pork	¼-inch lengths
5 tablespoons oil	4 tablespoons soy sauce
2 large eggs, beaten	¼ teaspoon salt

123 Heat pan, add oil, and sauté rice 2 minutes. Add eggs and mix well ½ minute. Add roast pork, onions, soy sauce, and salt. Sauté 1 minute. Serves 6.

FRIED RICE AND SHRIMPS

蝦
仁
炒
飯

4 cups cooked rice
1 cup diced shrimps (canned)
4 tablespoons oil
½ cup shredded onions

3 tablespoons oyster sauce
¼ teaspoon salt
3 eggs, beaten

Heat pan, add oil, and sauté shrimps and onions 1 minute. Add rice, oyster sauce, and salt. Stir 2 minutes. Add eggs, mix well, and sauté ½ minute. Serves 6.

RICE CONGEE WITH CHICKEN

鷄
粥

2½ cups rice
1 fryer (3½ pounds)
21 cups water

5 teaspoons salt
2 teaspoons gourmet powder
1 head lettuce shredded

Wash rice. Place in a large pot, add water, cover, and bring to a boil. Add whole chicken, cover, and simmer 1½ hours. Remove chicken. Remove meat from bones and shred. Add shredded chicken, salt, and gourmet powder to rice gruel and bring to a boil. Mix well and serve with shredded lettuce.

RICE GRUEL

白
粥

Plain rice gruel is to the Chinese breakfast what cereal is to the American breakfast. It is usually served with scrambled eggs, pickled or salted vegetables, or the so-called "thousand-year-old eggs" (page 29). In the recipe below, 1 cup of finely shredded chicken, beef, fish, or pork may be added to the gruel after it has simmered 15 minutes.

1 cup rice
7 cups water

2 tablespoons soy sauce
½ teaspoon salt

Wash rice and add water. Bring to a boil and simmer 25 minutes. Add soy sauce and salt just before serving. If a thicker gruel is desired simmer 10 minutes longer before adding the salt and soy sauce. Serves 3.

RICE GRUEL WITH BEEF

牛
肉
粥

1 cup rice
7 cups water
1 cup sliced beef

¼ cup shredded onions
2 tablespoons oyster sauce
1 teaspoon salt

Wash rice and add water. Bring to a boil and simmer 20 minutes. Add sliced beef and onions and simmer 10 minutes. Stir in the oyster sauce and salt. Serves 3.

RICE GRUEL WITH FISH CAKE, PORK AND LIVER

三
及
第
粥

2½ cups rice
1 tablespoon oil
1 pound chopped pork
1 pound fish cake
1 pound sliced pork liver
1 pound sausage covering
Salt as directed
Pork bones

MIX: 1 tablespoon cornstarch
1 tablespoon sugar
1 tablespoon crushed
fresh ginger
1 tablespoon crushed
garlic
2 tablespoons soy sauce

Wash rice thoroughly. Add oil and ¾ tablespoon salt and mix well. Bring 6 quarts of water to a boil, add rice and pork bones, and simmer 30 minutes.

Marinate sliced liver 15 minutes in mixture of cornstarch, sugar, ginger, garlic, and soy sauce. Bring 3 cups of water to a boil, add liver, and simmer 3 minutes. Remove.

Wash sausage covering by forcing water through it. Put it in a bowl, add 2 tablespoons salt, mix well, and let stand 15 minutes. Cut off excess fat and wash again by forcing water through it. Run 2 cloves of garlic through the sausage covering twice. Rinse. Bring 5 cups water to a boil, add sausage covering, and simmer 8 minutes. Remove and wash as before.

Add sausage covering and pork to the rice and simmer 50 minutes. Drop fish cake by tablespoonfuls into boiling rice gruel and simmer gently for 5 minutes. Remove sausage covering and cut into ½-inch lengths. Return to rice gruel. Add sliced liver and simmer 1 minute. Serves 8.

TURKEY BONES AND RICE CHOWDER

火
鷄
骨
粥

Turkey bones
14 cups water
2 cups rice
3 teaspoons salt
2 tablespoons soy sauce

Wash rice 4 times. Put turkey bones in a large pot, add water and rice, and bring to a boil. Simmer over medium heat 20 minutes, then over low heat 50 minutes, stirring occasionally after the first half hour to prevent burning. Remove bones. Add salt and soy sauce. Serves 8.

STEAMED RICE

This is the most economical way to prepare rice.

1½ cups rice
1½ cups water

Wash rice in cold water 4 times. Put in Chinese steaming bowl, add water, and steam 60 minutes. Rice will be dry and fluffy. Serves 4.

NOODLES & BUNS

麵
與
麵
包

Noodles, cakes, buns, and doilies are among the many flour products made from wheat and other grains.

Noodles are made of eggs and water combined with wheat, rice, or bean flour. They are sold fresh, dried, or fried, and come in every imaginable shape, in many degrees of thickness, and in various colors — some "cellophane noodles" are even transparent. Rice flour noodles are small and thin and are sold dried. Those made of beanstarch are transparent, thin, crisp, and dry.

Noodles may be served fried, in soup, or cooked either in a sauce of their own or the sauce resulting from the preparation of another dish. They are filling, go well with almost any food, and are frequently served on festive occasions such as birthday parties. They are a symbol of long life, and the extent of a guest's good wishes is measured by the quantity of noodles he consumes.

During the mid-spring festival, when the Great Dragon, ruler of the Empire of Worms, awakens the hibernating insects and calls them forth from their cocoons, long thin dragon-whisker noodles are eaten, and in the women's quarters all needlework is stopped lest one of them accidentally pierce the eye of the Great Dragon, and thereby delay the coming of spring.

Cakes in various sizes and shapes are baked and exchanged on all sorts of occasions. During the mid-spring festival, for instance, thin dragon-scale cakes are exchanged and sun cakes made of rice flour and imprinted with the image of a rooster, since the rooster is believed to inhabit the sun. During the mid-autumn festival moon cakes, round as the moon and sometimes a foot or two across are set out with melons and other round fruits

127

as sacrifices to the moon goddess, Ch'ang O. Ch'ang O is the wife of the sun god and they meet once a month, at the time of the full moon. Decorative moon pictures are set up in the courtyard and above the paper moon is a picture of the moon goddess. Beneath the goddess, in the disc of the moon, is the Taoist jade rabbit, who stands, pestle in hand, grinding up the elixir of life. Also represented is the woodsman eternally cutting at the cassia tree. Since the cassia tree is a giver of life, it repairs its wounds and the woodcutter's task is never done. When the moon rises the moon picture is burned along with incense and "spirit money" for the dead. Some then eat their moon cakes, others save them till New Year's Eve.

Buns made of flour, yeast or baking powder, and water are usually steamed. They may be filled with a sweet filling and served with tea or with a salty filling and served with the meal. Plain ones are frequently made in the shape of a peach, symbolizing the magic peach of immortality which the God of Long Life eternally holds in his hand.

Doilies are thin sheets of dough used in the making of wun tun and dumplings. They may be made at home or bought inexpensively at a Chinese grocery store or restaurant.

EGG NOODLES

蛋
麵

2 cups flour	3 teaspoons water
½ teaspoon salt	(if needed)
4 eggs	5 tablespoons cornstarch

Add salt to flour. Add unbeaten eggs and work well into flour. If too dry, add water, 1 teaspoon at a time. Sprinkle board with cornstarch (1 tablespoon) and roll dough paper thin. Cover the dough with layer of cornstarch and roll up on rolling pin. Press with the palms of the hands. Remove from rolling pin and roll again. Repeat process 3 or 4 times, using all of the cornstarch. Remove from rolling pin, fold, and cut into fine strips.

CHINESE BUNS

饅
頭

Chinese buns may be served plain or they may be filled with a sweet or a salty filling. The sweet filling may be bought at a Chinese cake shop or made at home according to the recipe given below.

1⅞ cups lukewarm water	1 tablespoon oil
½ cake yeast	1 teaspoon salt
1 tablespoon sugar	5¾ cups flour

Soften yeast in 2 tablespoons of lukewarm water. Put the rest of the water in a large mixing bowl and add sugar, oil, and salt. Add yeast mixture. Add half of the flour and knead well. Add remaining flour gradually and knead to a dough that will not stick to the hands. Remove and knead on a floured board for 2 minutes. Place in greased bowl. Cover and let rise until double in bulk (2 hours). Knead down and divide into 16 pieces. Form each piece into cap shape, fill with 1½ teaspoons filling, and close edges so that all of the filling is covered. Let rise 1 hour. Place on squares of oiled paper and steam 20 minutes.

SWEET FILLING

10 ounces azuki beans
8 cups water

4 tablespoons oil
⅔ cup brown sugar

Add water to beans and bring to a boil. Simmer 2 hours, or until tender. (There should be about ½ cup water left.) Mash beans through sieve. Heat pan, add 4 tablespoons oil, and sauté bean mash ½ minute. Add sugar and sauté 1 minute, stirring constantly.

SALTY FILLING

1 cup diced red roast pork
3 tablespoons green onions,
    cut in ½-inch lengths

1 tablespoon soy sauce
¼ teaspoon 5-spice

Combine ingredients and mix well.

LAYER BUNS

饅
頭
包

Follow the recipe for Chinese Buns to the point where the dough has been divided into buns. Flatten each bun, rub both sides with oil, and arrange in piles of 5 each. Roll out a larger piece of dough, rub with oil, and wrap around a pile of buns. Repeat until dough is used. Place bundles on pieces of oiled paper and steam 15 minutes.

CORNMEAL BUNS

蒸
窩
頭

1 cup flour
2 teaspoons baking powder
1 cup cornmeal

½ cup sugar
½ cup water

Sift flour. Add baking powder, cornmeal, and sugar. Mix well and add water. Knead and shape into buns about 3 inches in diameter. Steam 20 minutes.

STEAMED BUNS

蒸
飽

2 cups flour
4 teaspoons baking powder

1 cup water

Mix baking powder with flour and add water. Knead well and shape into buns about 3 inches in diameter. Steam 20 minutes.

STUFFED TAOFU

釀
豆
付

2 blocks taofu
½ cup dried shrimps
8 water chestnuts
1 egg
½ pound ground pork
¼ cup green onions, cut in
   ⅛-inch lengths
1 teaspoon salt
2 tablespoons soy sauce
1 tablespoon sherry

Few grains pepper
MIX: 2 teaspoons fresh ginger
   juice
1 tablespoon crushed
   preserved black
   beans
2 cloves garlic, crushed
1 tablespoon sherry
1 tablespoon soy sauce
⅓ cup water
1 teaspoon cornstarch

Cut taofu into pieces 1½ inches square and 1 inch thick. Soak shrimps in ½ cup cold water 30 minutes. Drain and mince. Peel water chestnuts and mince. Beat egg with fork until lemon-colored. Combine shrimps and pork and mix well. Add water chestnuts, egg, onions, salt, soy sauce, sherry, and pepper and mix well. Slit each piece of taofu, leaving about ½ inch uncut, and fill with 2 tablespoons of filling. Arrange in large bowl. Pour mixture of ginger juice, black beans, garlic, sherry, soy sauce, water, and cornstarch over taofu and steam 35 minutes. Serves 6.

One cup fresh shrimps, shelled and minced, or ½ cup fish cake may be used instead of dried shrimps.

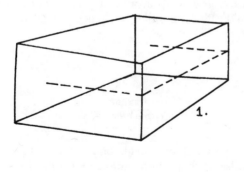

COOLIE PANCAKES

包
餅

2 cups flour
⅔ cup water
1 tablespoon oil
1½ teaspoon salt

⅓ cup green onions, cut in
    1-inch lengths
1 tablespoon chopped dried
    shrimps

Add water to flour and knead well. Sprinkle board with flour and roll dough to ¼-inch thickness. Rub surface of dough with oil, sprinkle with salt, and spread with onions and shrimps. Roll up like a jelly roll and cut crosswise into 2-inch pieces. Twist the ends of each piece, flatten, and roll to ¼-inch thickness. Cook on hot griddle until slightly brown on both sides.

PEKING DOILIES

薄
餅

Peking doilies are similar to Mexican tortillas. Fried in two thin layers, they can be pulled apart, spread with the desired sauce and filling, and eaten as a kind of rolled sandwich. The various sauces and fillings are arranged on the table and the Peking doilies served hot. Each guest spreads his own.

5 cups flour
1 teaspoon salt

2 cups boiling water
½ cup oil

Combine salt and flour and add boiling water, 1 cup at a time. Remove dough to table and knead thoroughly. Form into rolls about 2 inches in diameter. Cut crosswise into 1-inch pieces. Roll each piece to about ¼-inch thickness. Rub with oil and sprinkle lightly with flour. Put two pieces together and roll paper thin. Fry over medium heat until light brown on both sides. Roll doilies, place in bowl, and cover to keep warm. When all are fried, steam 3 minutes and serve hot.

SAUCES

Hoisin Sauce, Lemon Sauce, and Plum Sauce.

FILLINGS

Finely shredded roast duck, boiled ham, or plain omelet.
Thinly sliced boiled chicken, red roast pork, or cucumbers.
Parboiled bean sprouts, spinach cut in 2-inch lengths, onion tops cut
    in 2-inch lengths, or celery cabbage shredded.

FRIED NOODLES (CHOW MEIN)

炒
麵

1 pound homemade noodles
4 cups oil

Heat pan, add oil, and deep fry noodles until crisp. Remove to platter.

GRAVY

2 tablespoons cornstarch
2½ cups chicken broth
1 tablespoon sherry

2 tablespoons soy sauce
1 tablespoon sugar
1 teaspoon gourmet powder

Mix cornstarch with chicken broth. Add other ingredients and mix well. Bring to a boil and simmer 5 minutes.

GARNISH

½ pound pork, shredded
½ tablespoon soy sauce
½ teaspoon red coloring
1 tablespoon sugar
2 tablespoons oil
2 eggs
1 cup shredded celery
1 cup shredded string beans

1 cup shredded red peppers
1 cup Chinese peas
½ cup shredded onions
½ cup gravy
1 can mushrooms (4 ounces),
    shredded
½ cup shredded boiled ham
Parsley

Combine soy sauce, red coloring, and sugar, add to pork, and let stand. Beat eggs with fork until lemon-colored. Heat pan, add 1 tablespoon oil, and fry half of the beaten eggs in a very thin omelet. Repeat. Cut the omelets into fine strips. Drop celery, string beans, and red peppers in 2 cups boiling water and parboil 1 minute. Drain, saving the water.

Heat pan, add 3 tablespoons oil, and sauté celery, string beans, peppers, Chinese peas, and onions 1 minute. Add ½ cup gravy and simmer 1 minute. Reheat pan, add 1 tablespoon oil, and sauté mushrooms ½ minute. Remove. Reheat pan, add 2 tablespoons oil, and sauté pork 1½ minutes.

Garnish noodles with cooked vegetables, pork, shredded ham, shredded omelet, mushrooms, and parsley. Pour hot gravy over noodles. Serves 4.

If packaged noodles are used instead of homemade noodles they should be dropped in boiling water, cooked 2 minutes, and drained well before deep frying.

Dried mushrooms may be used instead of canned mushrooms, breast meat of chicken instead of pork, and any combination of vegetables, keeping in mind the quantity (5 cups), time required for parboiling (page 17), and color combination.

DESSERTS

甜
品

East and West differ both as to what constitutes a dessert and as to when it should be eaten. The Chinese do not serve a dessert at the end of the meal as the final triumphant course, but fit it in somewhere after the middle. It may come as late as the next to the last course, but is always followed by at least one major dish, such as steamed duck or fish. In ordinary family meals there is usually no dessert.

Chinese desserts are not always what they seem to the Westerner. Biting into what looks like a sweet cookie, he is often surprised to find it salty or bitter or filled with bits of vegetable and meat. Confucius, who was an epicure as well as a philosopher, claimed that every meal should have a combination of five flavors — sweet, sour, peppery, bitter, and salty. Some of the main dishes are partly sweet — Sweet-Sour Spareribs, for instance — and the need is not felt for a completely sweet one at the end of the meal. To the Chinese palate, a course with no other flavor than sweetness is insipid, too much of a good thing.

Since there is no oven in the average Chinese home, most pastries are bought from cake shops. Many kinds of steamed cakes are made at home, however. The Chinese also eat candied foods but do not confine themselves to fruits and nuts. A plate of sweets set on the table at the end of a meal will contain such items as candied carrots, lotus root, melon rind, coconut, ginger, squash, and tomatoes.

Fruit "teas" or "soups" are another favorite dessert. These are liquid, thickened with mochi flour (or cornstarch if mochi flour is not available) and served hot in soup bowls with porcelain spoons. Almond tea is a favorite, and two recipes are given here, one made with almond paste and the other with almond powder. Either provides a typical Chinese "tea" and is highly nutritious. Freshly ground almond paste may be bought at a Chinese restaurant or noodle shop and the canned almond powder is imported from the Orient.

ALMOND COOKIES

杏
仁
餅

Almond cookies are a favorite sweet and are served either at the end of the meal, between meals, or with afternoon tea. They may be baked plain or decorated with blanched almonds. For celebrations a drop of red coloring is put in the center of each cookie, signifying joy and good fortune.

3 cups flour
1 teaspoon soda
½ teaspoon salt
1 large egg
1 teaspoon almond extract

1 cup sugar
1⅓ cups shortening
Blanched almonds or
    red coloring

Sift flour, soda, and salt together. Beat egg with fork until lemon-colored. Add almond extract. Cream sugar and shortening well, add egg, and mix thoroughly. Add dry ingredients gradually. Roll into balls about 1 inch in diameter and place an inch apart on greased cookie sheet. Press thumb gently in center of top of each ball. Fill depression with half a blanched almond or touch it with the end of a chopstick dipped in red coloring. Bake 12 minutes at 350° F. This recipe makes about 54 cookies.

ALMOND TEA I

杏
仁
茶

1 can almond powder
    (4 ounces)
2 tablespoons cornstarch
1 cup sugar
1 can condensed milk
    (13 ounces)

6 cups water
½ cup blanched almonds,
    cut into ½-inch pieces

Mix almond powder, cornstarch, and sugar. Add milk and water gradually, mixing well. Bring to a boil and simmer 10 minutes. Stir in almonds and serve hot. Serves 10.

ALMOND TEA II

杏仁茶

1 quart fresh almond paste	6 cups water
1½ cups sugar	½ cup blanched walnuts,
1 quart fresh milk	broken into small pieces

Put almond paste in top of double boiler and add sugar. Add milk and water and bring to a boil over direct heat. Place in double boiler and simmer 10 minutes. Beat to smooth consistency with egg beater (about 3 seconds). Simmer 20 minutes. Stir in walnuts and serve hot. Serves 16.

AZUKI BEANS AND RICE

紅豆飯

| ½ cup azuki beans | 5 cups water |
| ¼ cup rice | 6 tablespoons sugar |

Wash rice 3 times. Wash beans and soak 6 hours in 1½ cups water. Drain. Place beans and rice in large pot and add 5 cups water. Bring to a boil and cook 1¼ hours. Add sugar and stir well. Serves 5.

CANDIED DATES

糖棗

| ½ pound dates | ¾ cups water |
| 1 cup sugar | ⅛ teaspoon cream of tartar |

Put each date on the end of an orange stick. Mix sugar and cream of tartar, add water, and stir over low heat until sugar is dissolved. Bring to a boil and cook until syrup threads when dropped from tip of spoon. Remove from heat. Dip each date in the syrup to cover, then place on oiled plate to cool.

CANDIED WALNUTS

合桃

Follow the above recipe for Candied Dates, using ½ pound shelled walnuts.

CANDIED LOTUS SEED TEA

子羹

| 1 cup candied lotus seeds | ¼ cup sugar |
| 1 tablespoon cornstarch | 3 cups water |

Mix cornstarch, sugar, and water. Bring to a boil and continue boiling 2 minutes. Add candied lotus seeds, simmer 3 minutes and serve hot. Serves 4.

135   Candied lotus seeds are sold at Chinese cake shops.

EIGHT PRECIOUS PUDDING

八
寶
飯

Eight objects, according to Chinese belief, when tied with the mystic knot, serve as charms to bring good and ward off evil. In ancient Peking on New Year's day the emperor would present to princes and important palace officials purses embroidered with the eight treasures, which were to be worn about the neck. The eight treasures differed according to religion and geography, but Eight Precious Pudding is a reminder of their power. The recipe given here is the authentic Peking recipe, and calls for some ingredients difficult to obtain—dragon-eye nuts, for instance. Any nut, candied fruit, or candied vegetable in the proper color, such as coconut, apricot, carrot, ginger, tomato, or Chinese melon may be substituted. The object is to make an attractive design around a red center in a variety of colors with light and dark alternating.

1½ cups mochi rice	1 cup blanched walnuts
6 cups water	36 raisins
½ cup sugar	1 dozen dried watermelon seeds
12 preserved dates, seeded	(shelled)
6 candied lotus seeds	6 candied red cherries
6 candied green plums	12 dragon-eye nuts, seeded

Bring rice and water to a boil and simmer over medium heat. Just before the water has completely evaporated stir well. (Mochi rice is very glutinous and quite different from ordinary rice.) Continue cooking until water has evaporated. Lower heat, add sugar, and mix well. Steam over low heat 2 minutes, or until rice looks firm and not watery.

Rub bowl 9 by 3 inches deep with butter. Cut the various fruits into ½-inch pieces. Arrange on bottom of bowl in 8 circles, the red fruit in the center surrounded by alternate rows of dark and light fruits. Add cooked rice, being careful not to disturb the pattern of fruits. Steam 30 minutes.

SAUCE

½ cup sugar
1 tablespoon cornstarch
1 cup water

Mix sugar, cornstarch, and water. Bring to a boil, and continue boiling 1 minute.

When rice is done, turn upside down on large serving platter. Lift off bowl and pour hot sauce over pudding. Cut with cake knife and serve hot. Serves 10.

EIGHT PRECIOUS TEA

八
寶
茶

12 pieces of each of these
candied foods: lotus root,
coconut, papaya, tomatoes,
Chinese melon, carrots
12 raisins

12 lychees
¼ cup sugar
3 cups water
½ teaspoon fresh lemon juice

Cut candied fruits into ¼-inch cubes. Shell lychee nuts, remove seeds, and break pulp into halves. Bring sugar and water to a boil, add fruits, and simmer 2 minutes. Add lemon juice. Serves 6.

Candied pineapple may be substituted for any of the candied fruits.

FRIED WALNUTS

炒
核
桃

1½ cups blanched walnuts
½ cup fine granulated sugar

2 cups oil

Pour 1 cup of boiling water over blanched walnuts and let stand 2 minutes. Drain and place on flat plate. Mix the sugar well into them and let stand overnight. Deep fry walnuts until they are golden brown.

GRAPE AND ORANGE TEA

蔔
萄
橙
羹

½ pound grapes
2 large oranges
¼ cup mochi flour

1 cup sugar
3⅛ cups water

Peel grapes and remove seeds. Peel oranges, separate into sections, remove membranes and seeds, and break into small pieces. Mix mochi flour and 5 teaspoons water. Form into small balls the size of a pea. Bring sugar and the rest of the water to a boil. Add flour balls and simmer 5 minutes. Add fruit, boil 2 minutes, and serve hot. Serves 4.

KANTEN

大
菜
糕

2 sticks white kanten
(agar-agar)
6 cups water

1½ cups sugar
2 teaspoons lemon extract
½ teaspoon red coloring

Rinse kanten slightly. Break sticks into small pieces and soak in 6 cups water 15 minutes. Add sugar and bring to a boil. Continue boiling until sugar and kanten are dissolved. Remove from stove and add coloring and lemon extract. Strain into 8-inch square cake pan and let cool. Place in refrigerator to chill. When it congeals, cut into 2-inch squares. Serves 6.

LOTUS SEED TEA

鮮
蓮
子
羹

1 cup fresh lotus seeds
3½ cups hot water
½ cup sugar

MIX: 2 tablespoons cornstarch
2 tablespoons water

Wash lotus seeds, cover with 2 cups water, bring to a boil, and continue boiling 5 minutes. Drain. Add 2 cups hot water, bring to a boil, and continue boiling 10 minutes. Drain. Peel skin from each seed, cut off both ends, and with a toothpick remove the green sprout inside the seed. (The green sprout is bitter and would spoil the taste.) Put seeds in bowl, add 1½ cups hot water, and steam 20 minutes. Transfer seeds and remaining water to a pan, add sugar and 2 more cups of water, and bring to a boil. Add mixture of cornstarch and water and stir until it thickens a little. Serve hot. Serves 3.

Sliced maraschino cherry or a few pieces of *san cha* (red cherry) may be added if desired.

NEW YEAR'S DUMPLINGS

元
宵
羹

FILLING

1 pound blanched walnuts
1 pound white sugar

1 pound sesame wafers
¾ cup lard

Break blanched walnuts into small pieces. Add 4 tablespoons sugar and mix well. Roll and grind sesame wafers to a fine powder. Rub the rest of the sugar into the lard until well blended. Add sesame powder and knead thoroughly. Roll into balls the size of a cherry and mold into cap shape. Fill center of each with a few pieces of sugar-coated walnuts. Close top and shape into round ball. Place on platter to harden.

Sesame wafers are sold in Chinese cake shops.

DUMPLINGS

Cold water

Mochi flour

Add cold water to mochi flour and knead well. If too soft, add more flour until it is the consistency of pastry dough. Form into balls, then mold each ball into cap shape. Put 1 ball of filling in each, close top, and shape into round ball, being careful that all of the filling is covered. Drop dumplings into boiling water, a few at a time, and continue boiling 3 minutes. After the first few seconds they will rise to the top; dislodge by stirring any that stick to the bottom of the pan. Serve hot, two or more in a bowl, with ½ cup of the water in which they were boiled.

NEW YEAR'S PUDDING

4 cups water
3½ cups dark brown sugar
2 pounds mochi flour

3 tablespoons oil
5 red dates
1 tablespoon sesame seeds

Stir water and sugar together over low heat until sugar is dissolved. Bring to a boil, remove from heat, and let cool. Add gradually to flour and mix well. Add oil and mix well. Pour mixture into pan or pyrex dish (about 8 inches in diameter and 3 inches deep) which has been lined with oiled ti leaves or dried bamboo leaves. Press dates into top and sprinkle with sesame seeds. Steam 3 hours.

ORANGE AND PINEAPPLE TEA

3 large oranges
1 cup pineapple tidbits
1 cup sugar

4 tablespoons mochi flour
Water as directed

Peel oranges with a sharp knife, cutting away the white covering of the fruit. Section the peeled orange by cutting on each side of the dividing membranes. Remove seeds and cut each section into 4 pieces. Place mochi flour in bowl and add 2 tablespoons water slowly. Make into 36 small round balls. Spread on a salad plate. Add sugar to 4 cups water and bring to a boil. Add the balls and simmer 2 minutes until the balls float. Add orange and pineapple tidbits. Simmer 1 minute. Serve in individual bowls with Chinese spoons. Serves 6.

ORANGE TEA

3 large oranges
½ cup sugar

2½ cups water
3 tablespoons mochi flour

Peel oranges with a sharp knife, cutting away the white covering of the fruit. Section the peeled orange by cutting on each side of the dividing membranes. Remove seeds and cut each section into 5 pieces. Mix sugar, mochi flour and water. Bring to a boil, add orange sections, and simmer 1 minute. Serves 3.

PINEAPPLE AND PEACH TEA

1 cup pineapple tidbits
2 large fresh peaches

¾ cup sugar
3 cups water

Peel peaches and cut into ½-inch cubes. Bring sugar and water to a boil, add fruits, and simmer 2 minutes. Serves 6.

RICE AND MUNGO BEANS

綠豆飯

¾ cup mungo beans
¼ cup rice

6 tablespoons sugar

Wash rice 3 times. Wash beans and soak 5 hours in 2 cups water. Drain. Place beans and rice in large pot, add 4 cups water, and bring to a boil. Cook 1 hour. Add sugar and stir well. Serves 4.

STEAMED DATE CAKES

蒸棗餅

2½ cups dried dates
1 cup water
1 tablespoon butter
1 cup mochi flour
1 tablespoon oil

⅓ cup sesame seeds
⅓ cup chopped walnuts
⅓ cup sugar
6 dried bamboo leaves,
    cut into squares

Wash dates thoroughly and bring to a boil in 1 cup water. Simmer until water has evaporated. Remove. Peel and remove pit. Put date pulp (there should be about 1 cup) in a bowl, add butter and mochi flour, and knead well. Form into balls, then flatten to cakes about 3 inches in diameter. Heat oil and fry sesame seeds 1 second. Remove. Mix chopped walnuts and sesame seeds and add sugar. Put 1 tablespoon of this filling in the center of each cake. Bring edges together and close at top so that a ball is formed. Press balls into carved wooden molds which have been dusted with flour. Remove cakes from molds, place on leaf squares, and steam 15 minutes.

STEAMED MOCHI DUMPLINGS

葉仔

This recipe may be made with either a salty filling and served with the main part of the meal or with a sweet filling and served as dessert.

½ pound mochi flour
½ cup water
Oil as needed

Ti leaves, cut into 12 strips
    about 9 x 3 inches

Mix flour, water, and 1 tablespoon oil to a soft dough. Separate into 12 balls and mold each one into cap shape. Fill center of each with a ball of desired filling. Bring edges together and close at top so that ball is formed. Oil the ti-leaf strips and place the filling at one end. Fold one edge in about 1 inch and roll. Place in bowl and steam 45 minutes.

SWEET FILLING

½ cup candied melon
½ cup candied coconut

1 tablespoon sesame seeds
2 tablespoons sugar

Mix ingredients and form into 12 balls.

SALTY FILLING

½ cup chopped roast pork
½ cup chopped shrimps
1 cup chopped water chestnuts
½ cup chopped bamboo shoots
1 tablespoon soy sauce

1 teaspoon salt
½ teaspoon gourmet powder
2 tablespoons green onions
1 teaspoon sherry
3 tablespoons oil

Mix ingredients well and form into 12 balls.

STEAMED SPONGE CAKE

蒸
蛋
餅

1 cup flour
½ teaspoon baking powder
5 eggs

¾ cup sugar
1 teaspoon lemon extract
1 cup soy bean filling

Sift flour and baking powder together twice. Separate eggs. Beat egg whites until they stand in peaks. Beat egg yolks with fork until lemon-colored. Add flour, sugar, baking powder, and lemon extract to egg yolks and continue beating until well blended. Gradually fold into egg whites. Pour half of batter into greased 8-inch square pan, spread with soy bean filling, and pour in the rest of the batter. Steam 1 hour.

Soy bean filling is made from soy beans and brown sugar and is sold in Chinese or Japanese cake shops.

SWEET PRETZELS

糖
環

1¾ cups cake flour
2 tablespoons sugar
½ teaspoon salt
3 eggs

1½ cups fresh milk
4 cups oil
MIX: ½ cup powdered sugar
½ teaspoon cinnamon

Sift the flour, sugar, and salt together. Beat eggs with fork until lemon-colored. Add flour and milk alternately to eggs, a small amount at a time, beating well. Heat oil and dip pretzel iron into hot oil, then into batter to fill the mold. Deep fry until pretzel is light brown. Remove from iron and drain. Sprinkle with powdered sugar and cinnamon. When cool store in airtight container.

TANGERINE AND PINEAPPLE TEA

波蘿橘子羹

3 large tangerines
1 slice pineapple
¼ cup mochi flour

¾ cup sugar
3⅛ cups water

Peel tangerines and separate into sections. Remove seeds and membranes and break each section into 5 small pieces. Cut pineapple into ¼-inch pieces. Mix flour and 5 teaspoons water. Form into small balls the size of a pea. Bring sugar and remaniing water to boil, add flour balls, and simmer 5 minutes. Add fruit, boil 2 minutes, and serve hot. Serves 4.

TASTY PRUNES

美味棗

1 pound prunes
2 tablespoons rock salt

8 tablespoons sugar
Juice of 4 lemons

Wash prunes and soak in 1½ cups water overnight. Drain and pack in Mason jar. Combine salt, sugar, and lemon juice and pour over prunes. Cover and let stand in the sun 2 weeks.

WALNUT AND DATE TEA

合桃棗羹

½ cup rice
3½ cups water
12 dates

1 cup blanched walnuts
½ cup sugar

Wash rice thoroughly and soak 10 minutes in ½ cup water. Remove seeds and boil dates 2 minutes in ½ cup water. Drain and force through sieve. Grind walnuts and rice together, adding water in which rice was soaked. Add sugar, date paste, and 3 cups water. Bring to a boil and continue boiling until slightly thickened, stirring constantly. Serve hot. Serves 5.

MENUS

菜
單

The following menus will serve four.

<table>
<tr><td>

I

Pork Hash and Eggs
Shrimps and Pineapple
Chicken and Sliced Vegetables
Red Roast Pork
Boiled Rice
Dessert—Almond Cookies
Tea—Lychee

</td><td>

II

Crab Omelet
Beef and Vegetables
Lion's Head
Pineapple Chicken
Boiled Rice
Dessert—Orange Tea
Tea—Jasmine

</td></tr>
<tr><td>

III

Walnut Chicken
Shrimps on Toast
Sweet-Sour Spareribs
Beef and Corn
Fried Rice
Dessert—Eight Precious Pudding
Tea—Rose Petal

</td><td>

IV

Lobster Tail Sautéed
Soy Sauce Chicken
Beef and Tomatoes
Pork, Fungi, and Eggs
Boiled Rice
Dessert—Sweet Pretzels
Tea—Chrysanthemum

</td></tr>
<tr><td>

V

Abalone Soup
Fried Noodles
Roast Duck
Paper-Wrapped Chicken
Sweet-Sour Fish
Beef and String Beans
Boiled Rice
Dessert—Eight Precious Pudding
Tea—Woo Loong

</td><td>

VI

Fish-Cake Soup
Steamed Pork
Chicken Thighs
Pumpkin
Boiled Rice
Dessert—Mochi Dumplings
Tea—Lychee

</td></tr>
</table>

An ordinary meal consists of not less than three dishes. When a recipe reads, "serves 4," it is assumed that there will be other dishes also.

MENUS

VII

Scallop Soup
Lemon Chicken
Sweet-Sour Fish Cake
Broccoli with Walnuts
Boiled Rice
Dessert—Orange and Pineapple
  Tea
Tea—Rose

VIII

Water Cress Soup
Drunken Chicken
Stuffed Cucumbers
Pickled Radishes
Boiled Rice
Dessert—Sesame-Seed Cookies
Tea—Woo Loong

IX

Stuffed Winter Melon (Soup)
Crisp Duck
Chicken with Fungi
Chow Fun
Boiled Rice
Dessert—Almond Jelly I
Tea—Jasmine

The following menu for a buffet supper serves sixteen.

Fried Rice and Ham,* page 123. (Multiply amounts by 4.)
Soy Sauce Chicken, page 75. (Multiply amounts by 3.)
Shrimps and Pineapple, page 59. (Multiply amounts by 2½.)
Barbecued Spareribs, page 91. (Multiply amounts by 2.)
Beef and Vegetables, page 89. (Multiply amounts by 3.)
Crab Omelet, page 42. (Multiply amounts by 3.)
Dessert—Almond Cookies
Tea—Lychee

* Plain rice may be substituted for fried rice.

At the request of the many pupils and friends who have enjoyed my Chinese cooking, I am including in the following pages thirty-eight new recipes developed in my classes and in my home since the earlier editions of this book were published.

February, 1964   *Mary Li Sia*

APPETIZERS

CURRIED BEEF WUN TUN

60 wun tun doilies
   (see page 27)
½ pound ground beef
8 water chestnuts
1 teaspoon fresh ginger juice
1 teaspoon salt

½ cup green onions, cut in
   ¼-inch lengths
1 teaspoon soy sauce
½ teaspoon gourmet powder
¼ teaspoon pepper
1½ teaspoons curry powder

Wash and peel water chestnuts and chop fine. Add beef, ginger juice, and green onions. Mix well. Add salt, soy sauce, gourmet powder, pepper, and curry powder. Mix. Spread doilies out on table and put ½ teaspoon of filling just below the center of each doily. Fold as shown in illustration on page 27. Deep fry until crisp.

SALTY PRETZELS

1 cup flour
1 cup cornstarch
1½ cups canned milk
¼ cup water
3 eggs, beaten

½ cup dried shrimps,
   chopped fine
1 teaspoon salt
6 cups oil

Mix flour and cornstarch. Add milk and water gradually. Add eggs and shrimps. Stir. Heat oil. Immerse rosette iron in oil until it is hot. Dip hot iron into batter to edge of rosette. When done, the flour will drop off the rosette iron. Allow to fry to light brown. Remove and drain. Repeat process until all batter is used.

SIU MAI

1½ cups ground pork
4 water chestnuts
4 tablespoons green onions,
    cut in ½-inch pieces
½ cup bamboo shoots,
    chopped
1 egg
1 teaspoon salt
1½ tablespoons soy sauce

2 tablespoons sherry
1 teaspoon sugar
1½ tablespoons cornstarch
¼ teaspoon pepper
¼ teaspoon gourmet
    powder
32 wun tun doilies
    (see page 27)

Wash, peel, and chop water chestnuts. Place ground pork in bowl; add water chestnuts, egg, salt, soy sauce, sherry, sugar, cornstarch, pepper, and gourmet powder. Mix well. Fill centers of wun tun doilies with 2 teaspoons of mixture. Gather doily about the mixture, leaving top open. (Be sure to dampen hands slightly when gathering doilies.) Place in steamer and steam 20 minutes.

SAUCE

1 teaspoon mustard
1 teaspoon boiling water

1 teaspoon vinegar
2 teaspoons soy sauce

Add boiling water to mustard and mix well. Add vinegar and soy sauce and stir well.
    To serve: Dip Siu Mai in sauce.

SOY SAUCE RADISHES

2 cups radishes
2 teaspoons salt
½ cup soy sauce

1 teaspoon sugar
½ teaspoon sesame oil
    (optional)

Wash radishes. Crush slightly and place in bowl. Add salt and let stand 15 minutes. Pour off excess water. Bring soy sauce, sugar, and sesame oil to a boil. When cool, pour over radishes and let stand 2 days. Remove radishes from sauce and serve.

SOUPS

FISH-CAKE SOUP

½ cup fish cake
4 water chestnuts
2 tablespoons green onions,
    cut in ¼-inch lengths

4 cups chicken stock
1 egg, beaten
Salt to taste

Wash and peel water chestnuts and chop fine. Add water chestnuts, green onions, and egg to fish cake. Heat chicken stock to boiling point. Add fish-cake mixture, a teaspoonful at a time, until all is used. Bring to a boil and simmer 10 minutes. Serve.

SCALLOP SOUP

1 cup dried scallops
1 cup bamboo shoots, sliced
    fine
¾ cup pork, sliced fine
3 eggs, beaten
2 teaspoons monosodium
    glutamate
Salt to taste

MIX: 2 tablespoons
    cornstarch
3 tablespoons water

Wash scallops and put in saucepan. Add 3 cups water and let soak 2 hours. Add 6 cups warm water. Bring to a boil and simmer 1 hour. Stir until scallops break up into fine shreds. Add bamboo shoots and pork. Simmer 15 minutes. Bring to a boil and add beaten eggs, cornstarch mixture, and salt. Stir 1 minute. Serves 6.

EGGS

HO PAO EGGS

10 eggs, beaten lightly
½ pound shrimps
1 cup pork, ground
10 water chestnuts
2 tablespoons green onions,
    cut in ¼-inch lengths

2 teaspoons sherry
3 tablespoons soy sauce
1 teaspoon salt
⅛ teaspoon pepper
Oil as directed

Shell shrimps and clean. Wash well and mince. Wash and peel water chestnuts and chop fine. Place pork in bowl and add shrimps, water chestnuts, green onions, sherry, soy sauce, salt, and pepper. Mix well. Heat pan, add 3 tablespoons oil, and sauté pork mixture 2 minutes. Remove. Reheat pan. Add 1 tablespoon oil, then 1 tablespoon of beaten egg. When lightly cooked, quickly place 1 teaspoon of the shrimp mixture on the left half of the omelet. Fold over immediately to seal the omelet. Brown both sides and remove to platter. Add oil and repeat process until egg and filling are all used.

SEA FOOD

SWEET-SOUR FISH CAKE

½ pound fish cake
2 tablespoons red roast
    pork, chopped
2 tablespoons ham, chopped

3 tablespoons green onions,
    cut in ½-inch lengths
3 water chestnuts
½ cup pineapple tidbits

Wash, peel, and chop water chestnuts. Pour fish cake in bowl and add chopped red roast pork, ham, green onions, and water chestnuts. Mix well. Heat pan and add oil. Spread fish-cake mixture in frying pan and brown both sides. Remove and cut into 1-inch strips; cut strips diagonally into ½-inch pieces. Place on serving plate and pour Sweet-Sour Sauce over it.

SWEET-SOUR SAUCE

1 tablespoon cornstarch	⅓ cup vinegar
2 teaspoons soy sauce	½ cup sugar
6 tablespoons pineapple juice	

Add soy sauce and pineapple juice to cornstarch and mix well. Add vinegar and sugar and bring to a boil. Simmer 1½ minutes. Stir in pineapple tidbits and pour over fish cake.

FOWL

CHICKEN

CHICKEN, CELERY, AND LETTUCE SALAD

Breast meat of 2 chickens
1½ cups celery, sliced fine
3 cups lettuce, shredded
1 cup fried almonds or
    walnuts
2 teaspoons soy sauce
2 teaspoons sesame oil
¾ teaspoon salt
¼ teaspoon pepper

1 tablespoon cider vinegar
3 tablespoons oil

MIX: 1 tablespoon soy sauce
    ½ teaspoon salt
    ½ teaspoon sugar
    ¼ teaspoon 5-spice

Marinate chicken meat in soy sauce mixture 10 minutes. Blanch nuts, remove skins, and deep fry. Heat pan, add 3 tablespoons oil, and sauté chicken meat 2 minutes. Stir well. Remove and cut in slivers. Combine chicken, celery, and lettuce in bowl. Blend well the soy sauce, sesame oil, salt, pepper, and vinegar. Pour over chicken, celery, and lettuce. Mix. Garnish with nuts. Serves 4.

Salad oil may be substituted for sesame oil.

CHICKEN THIGHS

12 chicken thighs
⅓ cup tomato catsup
⅓ cup soy sauce
⅔ cup sugar
½ teaspoon salt

¼ cup sherry
2 teaspoons ginger juice
3 medium cloves garlic,
    chopped fine

Mix all other ingredients, then add chicken thighs and mix well. Let stand 2 hours. Remove chicken and place on baking rack over shallow, foil-lined pan. Bake at 350° F. for 45 minutes. After first 15 minutes use remaining sauce for basting.

Chicken drumsticks or wings may be substituted for thighs.

CHICKEN WITH FUNGI

1 chicken breast
1 cup fungi
3 eggs, beaten
1 onion, sliced (1 cup)
½ cup chives, cut in
    ½-inch lengths
1 teaspoon ginger juice
2 cloves garlic, crushed
Oil as directed

MIX: 2 tablespoons soy sauce
      2 teaspoons cornstarch
      ⅓ cup water

MIX: 1 tablespoon soy sauce
      2 tablespoons sherry
      1 teaspoon salt
      ½ teaspoon pepper
      1 teaspoon sugar

Remove skin of chicken breast. Cut meat into 1-inch strips and slice diagonally. Marinate in soy sauce, cornstarch, and water mixture. Place fungi in large bowl. Add 3 cups hot water and let soak 30 minutes. Wash thoroughly. Drain. Heat pan, add 2 tablespoons oil, and scramble eggs. Remove. Reheat pan, add 2 tablespoons oil, and sauté fungi, onions, and chives 1 minute. Add soy sauce, sherry, salt, pepper, and sugar mixture and stir 1 minute. Remove. Heat pan, add 2 tablespoons oil, and sauté chicken 1 minute. Add soy sauce, cornstarch, and water mixture. Stir ½ minute. Add sautéed fungi, onions, chives, and scrambled eggs. Stir 2 minutes. Serve.

CHICKEN WITH WATER CRESS

1 cup sliced chicken breast
6 cups water cress, cut in
   2-inch lengths
3 tablespoons oil

MIX: 2 tablespoons soy sauce
1 tablespoon sherry
1 teaspoon salt
2 tablespoons water

Heat pan, add oil, and sauté chicken 1 minute. Add mixture of soy sauce, sherry, salt, and water. Add water cress and mix well. Cook 2 minutes. Serve.

DRUNKEN CHICKEN

1 fryer (2 pounds, 10 ounces)
3 cups sherry
2 tablespoons ginger juice

2½ tablespoons salt
¾ cup green onions,
   cut in ½-inch lengths

METHOD I

Wash chicken and rub salt and ginger inside. Place the green onions inside the chicken. Bring sherry to a boil. Add chicken and simmer 35 minutes, turning the chicken after the first 15 minutes. Remove, cut into segments, and arrange on platter (see page 62). Pour hot sauce over chicken and serve.

METHOD II

Add salt, ginger juice, and green onions to 3 cups of water and bring to a boil. Add chicken and simmer 35 minutes. Remove chicken. When cool, cut into segments. Add sherry to chicken and refrigerate 2 days. Remove chicken and serve cold.

LEMON CHICKEN

3½-pound fryer
1 tablespoon dark soy sauce
1 cup chicken broth
Lemon slices

MIX: 2 teaspoons sherry
¼ cup lemon juice
¼ cup sugar
½ teaspoon gourmet
   powder

Rub chicken with dark soy sauce and place in casserole. Pour mixture of sherry, lemon juice, sugar, and gourmet powder over chicken. Let stand 20 minutes. Spread slices of lemon on chicken. Add chicken broth. Cover and bake at 380° F. for 50 minutes. Remove chicken, cut into serving pieces, and arrange on platter.

To roast instead of bake: Rub chicken with soy sauce and mixture of sherry, lemon juice, sugar, and gourmet powder. Spread with lemon slices. Place on rack over a baking pan with 3 inches of water in it. Roast at 350° F. for 30 minutes. Add what is left of the dark sauce mixture to the chicken broth and use for basting the chicken every 10 minutes.

DUCK

CRISP DUCK

1 duck (3 pounds, 3 ounces)
2 cups cornstarch
4 cups oil
2 teaspoons salt-and-pepper
   mixture (see page 19)

MIX: 1 tablespoon soy sauce
½ teaspoon salt

Cut duck into halves through center of back. Smear each piece with soy sauce and salt mixture. Place in bowl and steam 1 hour. Remove all bones. Rub cornstarch on all sides of duck pieces. Place in bowl and steam 20 minutes. Remove and let cool. Heat oil and deep fry pieces of duck. Cut into 1½-inch pieces. Sprinkle with salt-and-pepper mixture. Serve.

MEATS

BEEF

BEEF TONGUE

2½ pounds beef tongue
2 cloves garlic, crushed
1 tablespoon Chinese
   preserved black beans

2 tablespoons soy sauce
1 teaspoon salt
2 cups water
4 tablespoons oil

Bring 8 cups of water to a boil; add tongue and let stand 2 minutes. Remove. Repeat process 3 times. Slit the skin with a

154

knife and peel from tongue. Wash tongue thoroughly and dry with cloth. Heat pot, add oil, and sauté garlic and Chinese preserved black beans ½ minute. Brown beef tongue; add soy sauce and salt, and sauté 1 minute. Add water; cover and simmer 1½ hours, adding ½ cup water if necessary.

Two potatoes, peeled and quartered, may be added if desired during the last 30 minutes.

PORK

STEAMED PORK

¾ pound ground pork
1 salted egg
1 thousand-year-old egg
1 fresh egg
6 water chestnuts

¼ cup green onions
1 tablespoon soy sauce
2 teaspoons sherry
½ teaspoon salt

Wash, peel, and chop water chestnuts. Place pork in bowl. Clean and shell salted and thousand-year-old eggs. Separate yolks from whites of salted and fresh eggs. Remove the yolk of the thousand-year-old egg; chop blackened egg white and add to pork. Add the other two egg whites, water chestnuts, green onions, soy sauce, salt, and sherry. Mix well. Place the egg yolk of the salted and thousand-year-old eggs about ½ inch deep into the pork. Place the fresh egg yolk on top of the pork. The yolks should be about one inch apart. Steam 30 minutes. Serves 4.

This dish is called the Three Emperors, and has an interracial connotation, with yolks of three different colors.

VEGETABLES

BROCCOLI WITH WALNUTS

1 pound broccoli
1 cup walnuts
½ teaspoon salt
Oil as directed

MIX: 2 tablespoons oyster
    sauce
½ teaspoon sugar
2 teaspoons sherry
¼ cup broccoli water

Wash broccoli and peel stems. Slice broccoli diagonally. Bring 2 cups of water to a boil; add salt and broccoli. Simmer 1½ minutes. Drain, saving ¼ cup water. Pour 2 cups boiling water over walnuts and let stand 2 minutes. Remove to a bowl and cover with 1½ cups warm water. Remove skins from walnuts. Heat 2 cups oil. Add nuts and deep fry. Remove. Reheat pan, add 3 tablespoons oil, and sauté broccoli 1 minute. Add mixture of soy sauce, sugar, sherry, and broccoli water. Stir 1 minute. Garnish with crisp walnuts. Serves 2.

CRISP LONG RICE (BEAN THREADS)

1 bunch long rice   *4 cups oil*

Cut long rice into 4-inch lengths. Pull apart to loosen. Bring oil to 380° F.; drop in one half of the long rice. It will puff up into a fluffy white nest. If there is no sizzling sound immediately, turn it over for ½ minute. Remove. Use as a garnish on a platter of foods, alternating with a piece of Manoa lettuce. (See Garnishes, pages 19-20.)

Long rice is made from mungo beans, not from rice. It is a thrilling experience to watch it puff into a fluffy white nest.

EGGPLANT WITH SHRIMPS

2 eggplants (long variety)   *2 cloves garlic, crushed*
2 tablespoons small dried   *1 teaspoon ginger juice*
   shrimps   *½ teaspoon salt*
3 tablespoons soy sauce   *⅓ cup water*
3 tablespoons sherry   *3 tablespoons oil*
2 teaspoons sugar

Rinse shrimps in strainer. Soak in ⅓ cup water 15 minutes. Remove shrimps, saving water in which they were soaked. Wash eggplant and cut diagonally into slices 1-inch thick (4 cups). Heat pan, add oil, and sauté garlic and shrimps 1 minute. Add eggplant, soy sauce, sherry, sugar, ginger juice, salt, and the water in which the shrimps were soaked. Bring to a boil and simmer 4 minutes. Stir. Serves 4.

EGGPLANT WITH SHRIMP SAUCE

2 eggplants (long variety)
1 tablespoon soy sauce
2 tablespoons sherry
2 teaspoons sugar
1 tablespoon shrimp sauce
2 garlic cloves, crushed

1 tablespoon ginger, chopped
⅓ cup water
¼ cup green onions, cut in
    ¼-inch lengths
3 tablespoons oil

Wash eggplant and cut into ½-inch pieces. Heat pan and add oil. Add garlic and shrimp sauce; sauté ½ minute. Add eggplant, soy sauce, sherry, sugar, and ginger. Stir 1 minute. Add green onions and water. Simmer 4 minutes. Serves 4.

HOME-GROWN BEAN SPROUTS

½ cup mungo beans   2 cups water

Wash mungo beans and place in bowl. Add water and let stand 6 hours. Drain and wash clean. Place a damp cloth on the bottom of a round aluminum vegetable strainer (8 inches in diameter) and place this above a pot. Spread the beans on the cloth, cover with another cloth, and pour 2 cups of water over this. Pour off the water which drains through into the pot; cover the strainer with a lid and let stand in a dark place. Repeat process three times a day, morning, noon, and night, each time pouring off the water which drips through into the pot. The pot should be kept dry but the cloth covering the beans should remain damp. The lid should be kept on the strainer at all times. At the end of 4 days remove sprouts and wash several times, until the green hulls have separated from them.

LONG RICE WITH GROUND BEEF

2 bundles long rice
1 cup ground beef
2 cups bean sprouts
½ cup green onions or
    chives, cut in 1-inch
    lengths

1½ cups chicken stock
2 tablespoons oil
MIX: 2 tablespoons soy sauce
    1 tablespoon sherry
    1 teaspoon salt
    1 teaspoon sugar

Cut long rice into 4-inch lengths. Soak 15 minutes in 6 cups hot water. Drain. Heat pan, add oil, and sauté beef 1 minute. Add stock and soy sauce mixture. Bring to a boil, add bean sprouts and green onions, and stir 2 minutes. Serve.

Water may be substituted for chicken stock.

LONG RICE WITH PORK

1½ bundles long rice
1 cup ground pork
¼ cup dried shrimps
2 tablespoons oil
2 tablespoons green onions,
    cut in ¼-inch lengths

2 cups chicken stock

MIX: 2 tablespoons soy sauce
1 teaspoon sugar
1 tablespoon sherry
1 teaspoon ginger juice

Soak long rice in hot water 20 minutes. Drain. Cut into 4-inch lengths and place in bowl. Soak shrimps 15 minutes in 1 cup hot water. Remove and chop. Heat pan, add oil, and sauté pork ½ minute. Add shrimps. Add soy sauce, sugar, sherry, and ginger juice mixture. Stir 1 minute. Add chicken stock and bring to a boil. Add long rice and simmer 1 minute. Stir in green onions. Serve.

Water may be used instead of chicken stock.

For a description of long rice, see Garnishes, pages 19-20.

PICKLED GINGER

3 cups young ginger, sliced
4 cups water
1½ cups sugar

1¼ cups vinegar
1 teaspoon sesame seeds
2 teaspoons salt

Wash ginger and cut diagonally into ¼-inch thick slices. Place ginger in pot, add salt and water, and let stand 1 hour. Drain. Add 4 cups of water, bring to a boil, and simmer 20 minutes. Drain and repeat process twice. Put vinegar, sugar, and sesame seeds in pot and bring to a boil. Add ginger and simmer 20 minutes. When lukewarm, pour into a sterilized jar.

PICKLED RADISHES

4 cups radishes
3 teaspoons salt
2 teaspoons soy sauce
⅓ cup cider vinegar

½ cup sugar
1 teaspoon sesame oil or
   salad oil

Wash and peel radishes. Crush lightly. Place in a bowl and add salt. Mix well and let stand 45 minutes. Pour off excess water. Mix soy sauce, vinegar, sugar, and oil. Shake well and pour over crushed radishes. Chill 1 hour before serving.

PICKLED VEGETABLES

2 cups turnips, diced
2 cups cabbage, diced
2 cups young string beans
1 garlic, crushed

1 small red pepper, chopped
1 tablespoon salt
3 cups water

Wash string beans and remove ends and strings. Drop into boiling water, cook 1 minute, and remove. Put ingredients in bowl, pour 2 cups boiling water over them, and let stand 20 minutes. Pour into a glass jar, being sure that it is full to overflowing. Let stand 3 days. Remove vegetables and serve.

Note: The turnips and cabbage should be rather coarse. A tablespoon of ginger juice may be added if desired.

PUMPKIN

4 cups pumpkin, sliced
3 tablespoons oil
1 button garlic, chopped
1 tablespoon Chinese
   preserved black beans
1 teaspoon ginger juice
⅓ cup water

⅓ cup green onions, cut in
   ½-inch lengths
1½ tablespoons soy sauce
1 tablespoon sherry
1 teaspoon sugar
1 teaspoon salt

Peel pumpkin and cut into pieces 1 x 1½ inches. Heat pan, add oil, and sauté garlic and black beans ½ minute. Add pumpkin and stir 1 minute. Add ginger juice, green onions, soy sauce, sherry, sugar, and salt. Mix well ½ minute. Add water and simmer 2 minutes. Serves 3.

STUFFED CUCUMBERS

3 medium-sized cucumbers
1 cup ground pork
10 water chestnuts
½ cup fish cake
1 egg, beaten
½ cup green onions, cut
    into ¼-inch lengths
1 teaspoon salt

2 teaspoons sherry
1 tablespoon soy sauce
¼ teaspoon pepper

MIX: 2 tablespoons soy sauce
1 tablespoon sherry
2 teaspoons ginger juice
⅔ cup water

Wash and peel cucumbers. Cut into halves lengthwise and remove seeds. Wash and peel water chestnuts and chop fine. Place pork, water chestnuts, fish cake, egg, green onions, salt, sherry, soy sauce, and pepper in bowl. Mix well. Fill cucumber halves with this mixture. Cut into 3-inch lengths. Place in pan and add mixture of soy sauce, sherry, ginger juice, and water. Cover, bring to a boil, and simmer 25 minutes. Serve.

Dried shrimps may be substituted for fish cake. Soak shrimps in 1 cup hot water 15 minutes. Remove and chop fine.

STUFFED WINTER MELON

3½-pound winter melon
½ cup chicken meat, diced
6 water chestnuts
½ cup raw ham, diced
1 cup cooked barley
½ cup bamboo shoot, diced
½ cup gingko nuts, canned
1 can mushrooms (2 ounces,
    stems and pieces)

½ cup onion, diced
½ cup green onions, cut fine
⅓ cup dried lotus seeds
3 teaspoons salt
2 teaspoons monosodium
    glutamate
½ pound pork, diced
1 pound chicken bones
8 cups water

Wash melon and slice off top, beginning about one-quarter of the way down. Cut edges of the melon in zigzag pattern. Remove seeds and place melon in pyrex bowl, standing upright. Wash and peel water chestnuts and dice. Add 1 cup of water to lotus seeds, bring to a boil, and cook 5 minutes. Remove and peel. Combine all stock ingredients, bring to a boil, and simmer 30 minutes. Remove bones. Add all other ingredients to stock and simmer 15 minutes. Remove ingredients from stock and put in melon. (Save stock.) Place filled melon, still in its pyrex bowl, in a deep steamer or large pot with tight cover. Add water to the pot to three-fourths the depth of the pyrex bowl, cover tightly, and steam 2 hours. Check water level from time to time, adding more if necessary to keep it at three-fourths the depth of the pyrex bowl. Serve at the table, with a separate container of the hot stock.

To cook the barley: Soak ½ cup barley in 2 cups of water 2 hours. Bring to a boil and simmer.

RICE

TSUNG

½ pound belly pork
2 pounds mochi rice
3 teaspoons 5-spice
12 salted eggs

⅔ cup black-eyed beans
24 dried bamboo leaves
Salt as directed

Cut belly pork into 12 pieces, add 5-spice and 3 tablespoons salt, mix well, and let stand overnight. Wash mochi rice, add 5 cups of water, and let stand overnight. Wash black-eyed beans, add 2 cups of water, and let stand overnight. Wash bamboo leaves and soak in warm water ½ hour. Remove and dry well. Drain and wash rice, add 1 tablespoon salt, and mix well. Drain black-eyed beans. Peel salted eggs, separate whites from yolks, and cut yolks into halves.

Fold one bamboo leaf to form a "boat," as shown below, Steps 1, 2, and 3. Place 3 tablespoons of rice in the folded leaf, then a piece of pork, then half an egg yolk on either side of it. Add one tablespoon of black-eyed beans and cover this with 3 tablespoons of rice. Wrap another leaf around this to give depth (Step 4). Fold in the sides (Steps 5 and 6), then the ends (Step 7), and then tie into a neat bundle with string. When the 12 bundles are ready, place them in a large pot, cover with warm water to which 1 teaspoon of salt has been added, and bring to a boil. Simmer 3 hours, adding water if necesary to keep covered. Remove from pot, unwrap, and cut contents of each package into four pieces. Serve with soy sauce.

161

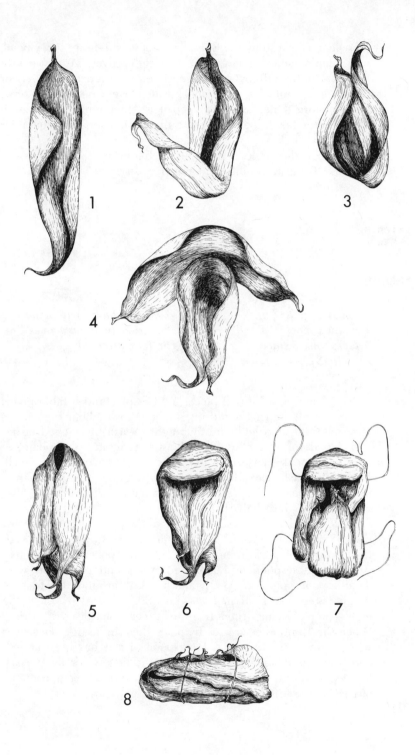

NOODLES

CHOW FUN

1 piece **look fun** *(rice flour noodles)*
4 cups bean sprouts
½ cup red roast pork, sliced
⅓ cup green onions, cut in ½-inch lengths
2 tablespoons oyster sauce
2 tablespoons oil

Cut *look fun* into ½-inch strips and unlace each strip. Heat pan, add oil, and sauté *look fun* and bean sprouts 2 minutes. Add green onions and oyster sauce and stir well 1 minute. Remove. Serves 3.

Soy sauce may be substituted for oyster sauce.

EGG NOODLES WITH BACON

1 pound egg noodles
1 pound bacon, cut in 1-inch lengths
12 ounces bean sprouts
½ cup green onions, cut in ½-inch lengths
⅓ cup oyster sauce
¾ teaspoon salt

Boil noodles 1½ minutes. Remove to pan of cold water. Drain. Heat pan, add bacon, and fry until crisp. Pour off 3 tablespoons bacon fat. Add noodles and bean sprouts. Stir 2 minutes. Add green onions, oyster sauce, and salt. Stir 1 minute. Serves 6.

Use egg noodles or T-top noodles (Hong Kong).

Chives may be substituted for green onions.

NOODLES WITH HOISIN SAUCE

14 ounces noodles or fine spaghetti
1½ cups ground pork
6 pieces salted turnips, chopped fine
2 cups peeled cucumbers, finely diced
4 cups bean sprouts
¼ cup chives
4 tablespoons Hoisin sauce
3 tablespoons oil
⅓ cup water
MIX: 1 tablespoon soy sauce
1 tablespoon sherry
2 teaspoons sugar
1 teaspoon gourmet powder
½ teaspoon salt

Bring 8 cups water to a boil. Add noodles and simmer 3 minutes. Drain, rinse in hot water, and place on platter. Pour 2 cups boiling water over bean sprouts and let stand 2 minutes. Drain. Heat pan, add oil and Hoisin sauce. Stir 1 minute. Add pork and sauté 1 minute. Add soy sauce mixture and chives, mix well, and cook 1 minute. Add ⅓ cup water and cook 2 minutes, stirring frequently.

To serve: Put individual servings of noodles in bowls. Add bean sprouts, cucumbers, and preserved turnips. Pour hot Hoisin sauce and pork mixture, over it and serve. Mix well with chopsticks before eating.

Note: Unlace the salted turnips and let stand 20 minutes. Wash before chopping.

DESSERTS

ALMOND JELLY I

1 stick white kanten
3 cups hot water
½ cup sugar
⅔ cup evaporated milk
1 teaspoon almond extract
2 cups fruit cocktail
   (No. 303 can; save syrup)

MIX: ½ cup fruit-cocktail
   syrup
¼ cup sugar
1½ cups water

Break kanten into small pieces and soak in 3 cups hot water 15 minutes. Stir. Add sugar. Bring to a boil and simmer until kanten is dissolved. Add milk and almond extract. Remove and strain into 8 x 8-inch pan. Place in refrigerator until firm. Cut into 1-inch squares and put in serving dishes, 6 to 8 pieces to a dish. Add 3 tablespoons fruit cocktail and 2 tablespoons of fruit-cocktail syrup mixture. Serves 5.

Canned chilled lychees, pineapple tidbits, mandarin oranges, or other fruits may be used.

ALMOND JELLY II

2 envelopes unflavored
    gelatin
1 cup cold water
2 cups milk, scalded
⅔ cup sugar
1 teaspoon almond extract
2 cups fruit cocktail
    (No. 303 can; save syrup)

MIX: ½ cup fruit-cocktail
    syrup
¼ cup sugar
1½ cups water

Place gelatin in bowl, add cold water, and mix well. Add sugar to hot milk and bring to a boil. Add to gelatin and stir well. Add almond extract. Pour into 8 x 8-inch pan and place in refrigerator until firm. Cut in 1-inch squares. To serve, follow directions for Almond Jelly I.

MOCHI DUMPLINGS WITH COCONUT

2 cups mochi flour
¾ cup shredded, sweetened
    coconut
¾ cup roasted peanuts,
    crushed

⅓ cup sesame seeds, toasted
¾ cup sugar
Water as directed

Put mochi flour in a bowl; add ¾ cup water to make a dough which is easy to handle. Shape dough into small marble-sized balls (about 72). Bring 6 cups of water to a boil. Drop in balls and bring to a boil again. Let simmer until balls float. Remove half of the balls to a platter. Sprinkle with half of the sugar, coconut, peanuts, and sesame seeds. Add another layer of dumplings and repeat. Serves 3.

This dish is served as dessert, frequently during New Year's festivities. The balls are symbolic of rounded happiness and luck; they carry the wish that the coming year will be sweetened with joy.

Mochi flour is known also as No Mai Fun.

SESAME-SEED COOKIES

1 cup shortening	2½ cups flour
1 cup sugar	½ teaspoon salt
1 egg, beaten	¾ teaspoon soda
¾ teaspoon vanilla	¾ cup sesame seeds

Cream sugar and shortening well. Add beaten egg and vanilla. Sift flour, salt, and soda together; add to creamed mixture. Mix well and form into small round balls. Roll balls in sesame seeds. Place each ball in the palm of the left hand, which is oiled, and flatten it to ½-inch thickness. Roll it in sesame seeds once more. Place on oiled cookie sheet and bake at 375° for 15 minutes. Makes 12 dozen cookies.

INDEX

索
引

167